# simply shetland

# simply

## shetland

It's a pleasure to launch our new company with the publication of our first project book of the same name, **simply** shetland.

In this book, you'll find beautiful examples of age-old, traditional Shetland knitting side-by-side with highly contemporary knitting projects. They share the common thread of pure Shetland wool, grown and spun in the Shetland Isles. Whether large or small—for the beginner or the advanced knitter—each project promises pleasure in the making with instructions that are carefully written and charted.

We've selected projects from some of our favorite designers, offering you a wide variety of both style and technique.

In addition to the knitting patterns, we always find interesting and fun things on our annual trips to Shetland. Last year was no exception and we report in this book on the unflappable joy of Wendy Inskter's **Burra Bears** and the interesting tale of the **Gunnister Purse** found in the Shetland Museum.

Enjoy our book. And more than this, enjoy the special and creative craft that is hand knitting.

# sweet violet jacket

*carol lapin*

## BACK

With US 5, CO 100 (110, 118, 126) sts. Work in garter st for 6 rows (3 garter ridges). Change to US 6 and work in st st, **AND AT SAME TIME**, inc 1 st at beg and end of next RS row, then every 8th row 4 (4, 5, 6) more times (110 (120, 130, 140) sts on needle).

<u>ALSO</u> <u>AT</u> <u>SAME</u> <u>TIME</u>, while continuing to inc at beg and end of row as established: on 20th, 38th, 56th and 74th rows (RS), purl the center 40 (44, 48, 52) sts (you'll have 4 purl ridges spaced 17 rows apart; later on, you'll pick up sts on these ridges to make ruffles).

Continue in st st until piece measures 20 (20, 20½, 20½)" from CO edge, ending with RS facing for next row.

**Next Row (RS):** K38 (43, 47, 52) sts and place on holder for right shoulder; BO 34 (34, 36, 36) sts for back neck; k38 (43, 47, 52) sts and place on holder for left shoulder.

## LEFT FRONT

With US 5, CO 33 (38, 41, 45) sts. Work in garter st for 6 rows (3 garter ridges). Change to US 6 and work in st st, **AND AT SAME TIME**, inc 1 st at *beg* of next RS row, then every 8th row 4 (4, 5, 6) more times (38 (43, 47, 52) sts on needle). Work in st st until piece measures 20 (20, 20½, 20½)" from CO edge. Place sts on holder for shoulder.

## RIGHT FRONT

With US 5, CO 33 (38, 41, 45) sts. Work in garter st for 6 rows (3 garter ridges). Change to US 6 and work in st st, **AND AT SAME TIME**, inc 1 st at *end* of next RS row, then every 8th row 4 (4, 5, 6) more times (38 (43, 47, 52) sts on needle). Work in st st until piece measures 20 (20, 20½, 20½)" from CO edge. Place sts on holder for shoulder.

## JOIN SHOULDERS

With RS's facing, join shoulders using 3-needle bind-off method.

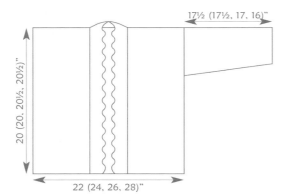

17½ (17½, 17, 16)"

20 (20, 20½, 20½)"

22 (24, 26, 28)"

## SLEEVES

Place marker 9 (9¼, 9½, 9¾)" down from shoulder seam on front and back. With US 6, pick up 46 (48, 50, 52) sts along armhole edge from marker to shoulder seam and 46 (48, 50, 52) sts from shoulder seam to marker (92 (96, 100, 104) sts on needle). Work in st st, **AND AT SAME TIME**, dec 1 st at beg and end of every 14th row 7 (7, 7, 7) times. Work without further shaping on rem 78 (82, 86, 90) sts until sleeve measures 16½ (16½, 16, 15)" from CO edge. Change to US 5 and work in garter st for 14 rows (7 garter ridges). BO.

## MAKE RUFFLES

*With circular US 5, RS of back facing and upside down, pick up 40 (44, 58, 52) sts in one of the purl ridges. Break yarn. Slide sts to opposite end of needle and reattach yarn.

**Row 1 (RS):** Knit, inc'g in every st.
**Rows 2, 4, 6, 8 & 10 (WS):** Purl.
**Rows 3, 5, 7, 9 & 11 (RS):** Knit.
**Row 12 (WS):** Knit.
**Row 13 (RS):** Knit.

BO.**

Rep from * to ** for rem 3 ruffles.

Sew sides of each ruffle to body.

## FRONT BAND

With US 5, CO 20 (20, 20, 20) sts. Work in garter st until piece fits comfortably along front edges and around neck (approx. 50 (50, 50, 50)"). BO. Sew band to body (make sure you have an equal number of garter ridges for each front).

## FRONT BAND RUFFLE

With circular US 6, RS facing, pick up 117 (117, 117, 117) sts up front edge to shoulder seam, 36 (36, 38, 38) sts along back neck and 117 (117, 117, 117) sts from shoulder seam down front edge (270 (270, 272, 272) sts on needle). Break yarn. Slide sts to opposite end of needle.

**Next Row (RS):** Knit, inc'g in every st.
**Next Row (WS):** Purl.

BO.

## FINISHING

Sew side and sleeve seams. Weave in ends. Block to finished measurements.

# sophia cardigan

*sandi rosner*

## MATERIALS

YARN: Jamieson's Shetland Double Knitting - 400 (450, 500) grams. Shown in Sunglow (185).
NEEDLES: US 4 (3.5 mm) and US 6 (4 mm), *or correct needles to obtain gauge.*
ACCESSORIES: Stitch holders. Six ¾" buttons.

## MEASUREMENTS

CHEST: 42 (46, 50)".
LENGTH*: 23 (23½, 24)".
SLEEVE LENGTH TO UNDERARM*: 17½ (17½, 18)".
SLEEVE LENGTH TO SHOULDER*: 22½ (22½, 23)".

*Measured from turning ridge or with cuff turned back at turning ridge.*

## GAUGE

On US 6 in st st: 22 sts and 30 rows = 4".

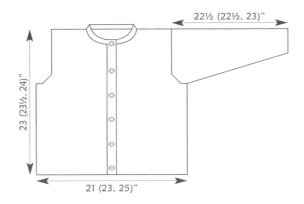

## BACK
### MAKE HEM FACING
With US 4, CO 111 (123, 135) sts. Work in st st for 10 (10, 10) rows, ending with WS facing for next row.

**Next Row (WS) (Turning Ridge):** Knit.

Change to US 6 and work as follows:

**Row 1 (RS):** K1; ([P1, k5] 18 (20, 22) times); end p1, k1.
**Row 2 (WS):** Purl.

Rep these 2 rows until piece measures 15 (15, 15)" from turning ridge, ending with RS facing for next row.

### SHAPE ARMHOLES
BO 5 (8, 11) sts at beg of next 2 rows, 2 (2, 2) sts at beg of next 4 (6, 8) rows, then dec 1 (1, 1) st at beg and end of every RS row 3 (4, 5) times, ending with RS facing for next row.

Work on rem 87 (87, 87) sts as follows:

**Row 1 (RS):** K2; ([yo, ssk, k1, k2tog, yo, k1] 14 (14, 14) times); end k1.
**Row 2 (WS):** Purl.
**Row 3 (RS):** K3; ([yo, sl1 kwise, k2tog, psso, yo, k3] 14 (14, 14) times).
**Row 4 (WS):** Purl.

Rep Rows 1-4 above until piece measures 8 (8½, 9)" from beg of armhole shaping, ending with RS facing for next row.

### SHAPE NECK AND SHOULDERS
**Next Row (RS):** BO 9 (9, 9) sts; work 19 (19, 19) sts as set; place rem 59 (59, 59) sts on holder.

Continue on right back only as follows:

**Next Row (WS):** P2tog; purl to end of row.
**Next Row (RS):** BO 9 (9, 9) sts; work 9 (9, 9) sts as set.
**Next Row (WS):** P2tog; purl to end of row.

BO rem 8 (8, 8) sts.

Rejoin yarn to sts on holder. BO 31 (31, 31) sts for back neck; work as set to end of row. Work on left back only, reversing shaping.

### RIGHT FRONT
#### MAKE HEM FACING
With US 4, CO 57 (63, 69) sts. Work in st st for 10 (10, 10) rows, ending with WS facing for next row.

**Next Row (WS) (Turning Ridge):** Knit.

Change to US 6 and work as follows:

**Row 1 (RS):** K2, yo, ssk, k1, k2tog, yo, k1; ([k5, p1] 8 (9, 10) times); end k1.
**Row 2 (WS):** Purl.
**Row 3 (RS):** K3, yo, sl1 kwise, k2tog, psso, yo, k2; ([k5, p1] 8 (9, 10) times); end k1.
**Row 4 (WS):** Purl.

Rep Rows 1-4 above until same length as back up to armhole, ending after working Row 4.

#### SHAPE ARMHOLE
Continuing as set, BO 5 (8, 11) sts at beg of next WS row, then 2 (2, 2) sts at beg of next 2 (3, 4) WS rows, then dec 1 (1, 1) st at armhole edge every other row 3 (4, 5) times, ending with RS facing for next row. Work without further shaping on rem 45 (45, 45) sts as follows:

**Row 1 (RS):** K2; ([yo, ssk, k1, k2tog, yo, k1] 7 (7, 7) times); end k1.
**Row 2 (WS):** Purl.
**Row 3 (RS):** K3, ([yo, sl1 kwise, k2tog, psso, yo, k3] 7 (7, 7) times).
**Row 4 (WS):** Purl.

Rep Rows 1-4 above until piece measures 5½ (6, 6½)" from beg of armhole shaping, ending after working Row 4.

#### SHAPE NECK
Continuing as set, BO 12 (12, 12) sts at beg of next RS row, then dec 1 (1, 1) st at neck edge every other row 7 (7, 7) times. Work without further shaping on rem 26 (26, 26) sts until same length as back up to shoulder. BO 9 (9, 9) sts at beg of next 2 (2, 2) WS rows. BO rem 8 (8, 8) sts.

### LEFT FRONT
#### MAKE HEM FACING
With US 4, CO 57 (63, 69) sts. Work in st st for 10 (10, 10) rows, ending with WS facing for next row.

**Next Row (WS) (Turning Ridge):** Knit.

Change to US 6 and work as follows:

**Row 1 (RS):** K1; ([p1, k5] 8 (9, 10) times); end k1, yo, ssk, k1, k2tog, yo, k2.
**Row 2 (WS):** Purl.
**Row 3 (RS):** K1; ([p1, k5] 8 (9, 10) times); end k2, yo, sl1 kwise, k2tog, psso, yo, k3.
**Row 4 (WS):** Purl.

Rep Rows 1-4 above until same length as back up to armhole, ending after working Row 4.

#### SHAPE ARMHOLE
Continuing as set, BO 5 (8, 11) sts at beg of next RS row, then 2 (2, 2) sts at beg of next 2 (3, 4) RS rows, then dec 1 (1, 1) st at armhole edge every other row 3 (4, 5) times, ending with RS facing for next row. Work without further shaping on rem 45 (45, 45) sts as follows:

**Row 1 (RS):** K2; ([yo, ssk, k1, k2tog, yo, k1] 7 (7, 7) times); end k1.
**Row 2 (WS):** Purl.
**Row 3 (RS):** K3; ([yo, sl1 kwise, k2tog, psso, yo, k3] 7 (7, 7) times).
**Row 4 (WS):** Purl.

Rep Rows 1-4 above until piece measures 5½ (6, 6½)" from beg of armhole shaping, ending after working Row 4.

#### SHAPE NECK
Continuing as set, BO 12 (12, 12) sts at beg of next WS row, then dec 1 (1, 1) st at neck edge every other row 7 (7, 7) times. Work without further shaping on rem 26 (26, 26) sts until same length as back up to shoulder. BO 9 (9, 9) sts at beg of next 2 (2, 2) RS rows. BO rem 8 (8, 8) sts.

### SLEEVES
#### MAKE HEM FACING
With US 4, CO 57 (63, 63) sts. Work in st st for 10 (10, 10) rows, ending with WS facing for next row.

**Next Row (WS) (Turning Ridge):** Knit.

Change to US 6 and work as follows:

**Row 1 (RS):** K1; ([p1, k5] 9 (10, 10) times); end p1, k1.
**Row 2 (WS):** Purl.

Work Rows 1-2 above, **AND AT SAME TIME,** inc 1 st at beg and end of every 6th row 18 (18, 20) times. Work without further shaping on rem 93 (99, 103) sts until piece measures 17½ (17½, 18)" from turning ridge.

### SHAPE SLEEVE CAP

BO 5 (8, 11) sts at beg of next 2 (2, 2) rows, 2 (2, 2) sts at beg of next 4 (6, 8) rows, then dec 1 (1, 1) st at beg and end of every other row 9 (12, 16) times. BO 2 (2, 2) sts at beg of next 10 (8, 2) rows, then 3 (3, 3) sts at beg of next 6 (4, 4) rows. BO rem 19 (19, 17) sts.

### FINISHING

*Sew shoulders together. Sew sleeves to armholes. Sew side and sleeve seams.*

### NECKBAND

With US 4, RS facing, pick up 29 (29, 29) sts up right neck edge to shoulder seam, 39 (39, 39) sts along back neck edge, and 29 (29, 29) sts from shoulder seam down left neck edge (97 (97, 97) sts on needle). Turn and work as follows:

**Row 1 (WS):** Purl.
**Row 2 (RS):** ([P1, k5] 16 (16, 16) times); end p1.

Rep Rows 1-2 above 3 (3, 3) more times.

**Next Row (RS) (Turning Ridge):** Knit.

Work in st st for 8 (8, 8) rows. BO loosely.

### BUTTONBAND

With US 4, RS facing, pick up 107 (107, 113) sts along left front edge, beg at turning ridge on neckband, and ending at turning ridge on bottom edge. Turn and work as follows:

**Row 1 (WS):** Purl.
**Row 2 (RS):** ([K5, p1] 17 (17, 18) times); end k5.

Rep Rows 1-2 above 3 (3, 3) more times.

**Next Row (WS) (Turning Ridge):** Knit.

Work in st st for 8 (8, 8) rows. BO loosely.

### BUTTONHOLE BAND

With US 4, RS facing, pick up 107 (107, 113) sts along right front edge, beg at turning ridge on bottom edge, and ending at turning ridge on neckband. Turn and work as follows:

**Rows 1, 3, & 7 (WS):** Purl.
**Rows 2, 6 & 8 (RS):** ([K5, p1] 17 (17, 18) times); end k5.
**Row 4 (RS) (1st & 2nd Sizes):** ([K5, p1, k1, BO 3, k1, p1, k5, p1] 5 (5) times); end k5, p1, k1, BO3, k1, p1, k5.
**Row 4 (RS) (3rd Size):** ([K5, p1, k5, p1, k1, BO 3, k1, p1] 6 times); end k5.
**Row 5 (WS):** P7; ([CO 3, p15] 5 (5, 5) times); end CO 3, p7 (7, 13).
**Row 9 (WS) (Turning Ridge):** Knit.
**Rows 10, 12 & 16 (RS):** Knit.
**Rows 11, 15 & 17 (WS):** Purl.
**Row 13 (WS):** P7; ([BO 3, p15] 5 (5, 5) times); end BO 3, p7 (7, 13).
**Row 14 (RS):** K7 (7, 13); ([CO 3, k15] 5 (5, 5) times); end CO 3, k7.

BO loosely.

Fold neckband to inside along turning ridge and sew down. Fold bottom edge to inside along turning ridge and sew down. Fold buttonband and buttonhole band to inside along turning ridges and sew down. Sew layers of buttonhole band together along edges of buttonholes. Weave in ends. Block to finished measurements. Sew on buttons opposite buttonholes.

# spectator jacket

*mari dembrow*

## MATERIALS
**YARN:** Jamieson's Shetland Double Knitting - 400 (400, 400, 450, 450, 450) grams MC; 100 (100, 100, 150, 150, 150) grams CC. Shown in MC, Sholmit (103) and CC, Shaela (102).
**NEEDLES:** US 3 (3.25 mm) and US 5 (3.75 mm), *or correct needles to obtain gauge.*
Size C crochet hook (optional).
**ACCESSORIES:** Stitch holders. Seven ½" buttons.

## MEASUREMENTS
**CHEST:** 42 (44, 46, 48, 50, 52)".
**LENGTH:** 22 (22½, 23, 23½, 24, 24½)".
**SLEEVE LENGTH** (MEASURED FROM TOP OF SHOULDER): 22 (22½, 23, 23½, 24, 24½)".

## GAUGE
In **Pattern Stitch:** 24 sts and 36 rows = 4".
In st st: 26 sts and 32 rows = 4".

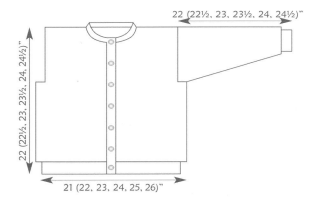

## ABOUT CHARTS
Read odd-numbered (RS) rows from right to left and even-numbered (WS) rows from left to right.

## W&T (WRAP AND TURN)
Shape sleeve cap using short rows. To prevent holes at turns, wrap a st at end of each short row as follows: where indicated, sl next st pwise, bring yarn to front, and sl slipped st back to left-hand needle. Turn and you're ready to work the next row.

## MAKE BUTTONHOLE
**Row 1 (RS):** P1, sl1, p1, k1, p1, sl1, k1, k1; pass the k st over the k st; k1; pass the k st over the k st; place last k st on left-hand needle; pass the sl st over the k st; return st to right-hand needle; p1, k1, p1, sl1, p1.
**Row 2 (WS):** K1, p1, k1, p1, k1, p1, CO 3, p1, k1, p1, k1, p1, k1.

## RIBBING STITCH
**Row 1 (RS) (1st, 3rd & 5th Sizes Back & All Sizes Sleeve Cuff):** *P1, k1, p1, sl1 wyib**; rep from * to ** to last st; p1.
**Row 1 (RS) (2nd, 4th & 6th Sizes Back):** *P1, k1, p1, sl1 wyib**; rep from * to ** to last 3 sts; p1, k1, p1.
**Row 2 (WS) (All Sizes Back & All Sizes Sleeve Cuff):** *K1, p1**; rep from * to ** to last st; k1.

Rep Rows 1-2.

## PATTERN STITCH (MULTIPLE OF 2 + 1)
**Row 1 (WS):** P1; *yo, sl1wyif, p1**; rep from * to **.
**Row 2 (RS):** *K1, knit the sl st and yo tog tbl**; rep from * to ** to last st; k1.

Rep Rows 1-2.

## BACK
With US 3 and CC, CO 125 (131, 137, 143, 149, 155) sts. Beg with Row 2, work **Ribbing Stitch** for 3 (3, 3, 3, 3, 3)", ending with RS facing for next row. Change to US 5 and MC. Leave 8' tail to sew or crochet sides tog.

**Next Row (RS):** Knit.
**Next Row (WS):** Change to **Pattern Stitch** and work until piece measures 13 (13½, 14, 14½, 15, 15½)" from CO edge, ending with WS facing for next row.

# spectator jacket

## SHAPE ARMHOLES

**Next Row (WS):** P14 and place on holder for left armhole; work to last 14 sts, place these on holder for right armhole.

Continue as set on rem 97 (103, 109, 115, 121, 127) sts until piece measures 22 (22½, 23, 23½, 24, 24½)" from CO edge, ending with RS facing for next row.

**Next Row (RS):** Work 30 (33, 36, 39, 42, 45) sts and place on holder for left shoulder, BO 37 (37, 37, 37, 37, 37) sts and place on holder for back neck, work 30 (33, 36, 39, 42, 45) sts and place on holder for right shoulder.

## LEFT FRONT

With US 3 and CC, CO 77 (81, 83, 85, 89, 93) sts.

**Next Row (WS):** *K1, p1**; rep from * to ** to last st; k1.

Work **Chart A** for 3 (3, 3, 3, 3, 3)", ending with WS facing for next row.

**Next Row (WS):** Work 15 sts and place on holder for left front band; work rem 62 (66, 68, 70, 74, 78) sts.

Change to US 5 and MC. Leave an 8' tail to sew or crochet sides tog.

**Next Row (RS):** Knit to last 2 sts, k2tog (61 (65, 67, 69, 73, 77) sts rem).

Work in **Pattern Stitch** until piece measures 13 (13½, 14, 14½, 15, 15½)" from CO edge, ending with WS facing for next row.

## SHAPE ARMHOLE

**Next Row (WS):** Work to last 14 sts and place these 14 sts on holder for left armhole.

Continue on rem 47 (51, 53, 55, 59, 63) sts until piece measures 18¼ (18¾, 19¼, 19¾, 20¼, 20¾)" from CO edge, ending with WS facing for next row.

## SHAPE NECK

**Next Row (WS):** P1, p2tog, p2, *yo, sl1wyif, p1**; rep from * to **.
**Next Row (RS):** Work to last 3 sts; k2tog, k1.

Rep these 2 rows until 30 (33, 36, 39, 42, 45) sts rem. Work without further shaping until piece measures 22 (22½, 23, 23½, 24, 24½)" from CO edge, ending with RS facing for next row. Work 1 row. Place shoulder sts on holder.

## LEFT FRONT BAND

Using CC, place 15 left band sts on US 3, and leaving an 8' tail, continue pattern as set until left band measures same as left front up to neck shaping, ending with RS facing for next row. Break yarn. Sew left band to left front, using tail.

## RIGHT FRONT

With US 3 and CC, CO 77 (81, 83, 85, 89, 93) sts.

**Next Row (WS):** *K1, p1**; rep from * to ** to last st; k1.

Work **Chart B** for 3 (3, 3, 3, 3, 3)", **AND AT SAME TIME, Make Buttonhole** beg on Row 8 (10, 10, 10, 14, 8), ending with WS facing for next row.

**Next Row (WS):** Work 62 (66, 68, 70, 74, 78) sts; place last 15 sts on holder for right front band.

Change to US 5 and MC.

**Next Row (RS):** K2tog, knit to end of row (61 (65, 67, 69, 73, 77) sts rem).

Work in **Pattern Stitch** until piece measures 13 (13½, 14, 14½, 15, 15½)" from CO edge, ending with WS facing for next row.

## SHAPE ARMHOLE

**Next row (WS):** P14 sts and place on holder for right armhole; work to end of row.

Continue on rem 47 (51, 53, 55, 59, 63) sts until piece measures 18¼ (18¾, 19¼, 19¾, 20¼, 20¾)" from CO edge, ending with WS facing for next row.

## SHAPE NECK

**Next Row (WS):** Work to last 4 sts; p1, psp, p1.
**Next row (RS):** K1, ssk, k1; work to end of row.

Rep these 2 rows until 30 (33, 36, 39, 42, 45) sts rem *(you will end on either a RS or WS row, depending on how many decs are worked for your size)*. Work without further shaping until piece measures 22 (22½, 23, 23½, 24, 24½)" from CO edge, ending with RS facing for next row. Work 1 row. Place shoulder sts on holder.

## RIGHT FRONT BAND

With CC, place 15 right band sts on US 3, and leaving an 8' tail, continue pattern as set, **AND AT SAME TIME, Make Buttonhole** every 3 (3, 3¼, 3¼, 3¼, 3½)". Work until right band measures same as right front up to neck shaping, ending with RS facing for next row. Break yarn, leaving a 5' tail to join shoulders to. Sew right band to right front, using tail.

## JOIN SHOULDERS
With RS's facing, join shoulders using 3-needle bind-off method.

## COLLAR
With US 3 and CC, RS facing, work 15 (15, 15, 15, 15, 15) right front band sts as set, pick up 40 (40, 40, 40, 40, 40) sts up right front neck, pick up 37 (37, 37, 37, 37, 37) sts along back neck edge, pick up 40 (40, 40, 40, 40, 40) sts down left neck edge, work 15 (15, 15, 15, 15, 15) left front band sts as set (147 (147, 147, 147, 147, 147) sts on needle).

**Next Row (WS):** *K1, p1**; rep from * to ** to last st; k1.
**Next Row (RS):** *P1, sl1, p1, k1**; rep from * to ** to last 3 sts; p1, sl1, p1.

Rep these 2 rows, **AND AT SAME TIME, Make Buttonhole** appropriately spaced from previous buttonhole. End with RS facing for next row.

BO as follows: ([BO 2 sts tog] 3 times), ([BO 3 sts, BO 2 sts tog] 10 times), BO 35 sts, ([BO 2 sts tog, BO 3 sts] 10 times), ([BO 2 sts tog] 3 times).

## SLEEVES
With US 5 and MC, RS facing, k14 (14, 14, 14, 14, 14) sts from holder; pick up 45 (45, 45, 45, 45, 45) sts from underarm up to shoulder seam and 45 (45, 45, 45, 45, 45) sts from shoulder seam down to underarm, k14 (14, 14, 14, 14, 14) sts from holder (118 (118, 118, 118, 118, 118) sts on needle).

**Next Row (WS):** P78, W&T.
**Next Row (RS):** K38, W&T.
**Next Row (WS):** P40, W&T.
**Next Row (RS):** K42, W&T.
**Next Row (WS):** P44, W&T.

Continue in this manner until you have wrapped 6th purl from end. Turn; knit to end of row, working wraps tog with wrapped sts.

Continue in st st, **AND AT SAME TIME**, dec 1 st at beg and end of every 6th row 12 (10, 10, 8, 6, 4) times, then every 8th row 7 (9, 9, 11, 13, 15) times. Work without further shaping on rem 80 (80, 80, 80, 80, 80) sts until sleeve measures 19½ (20, 20½, 21, 21½, 22)" from top of sleeve cap, ending with RS facing for next row.

## DEC FOR CUFF
**Next Row (RS):** Change to US 3 and CC and dec as follows: k2tog, k1, k2tog ([k3, k2tog] 15 times) (63 (63, 63, 63, 63, 63) sts rem).

Beg with Row 2, work in **Ribbing Stitch** for (2½ (2½, 2½, 2½, 2½, 2½)", ending with RS facing for next row. BO.

## FINISHING
Sew sleeve and side seams. To make piping along sides, work a slip stitch in CC in each "V" of slip sts on pattern, beg at left front ribbing and working over shoulder down to left back ribbing. Next, start at right back ribbing; work over shoulder down to right front ribbing. Crochet sl st edge in CC around perimeter of sweater and collar. Weave in ends. Block to finished measurements. Sew on buttons opposite buttonholes.

## Chart A
**Left Front Ribbing**

## Chart B
**Right Front Ribbing**

## Key
k on right side rows; p on wrong side rows.
p on right side rows; k on wrong side rows.
sl1wyib.

*spectator jacket*

*hjaltland pullover*

# hjaltland pullover

*mari dembrow*

## MATERIALS

**YARN:** Jamieson's Shetland Double Knitting - 500 (500, 550, 600, 650) grams. Shown in Blue Lovat (232) on opposite page and on page 17. Shown in Sunrise (187) on page 24.
**NEEDLES:** US 3 (3.25 mm) and US 5 (3.75 mm), *or correct needles to obtain gauge.*
Size C Crochet hook (optional).
**ACCESSORIES:** Stitch holders. Two ¾" buttons.

## MEASUREMENTS

**CHEST:** 41 (43½, 46, 48, 50)".
**LENGTH:** 25½ (26, 26½, 27, 27½)".
**SLEEVE LENGTH:** 21 (21½, 21½, 22, 22)".

## GAUGE

On US 5 in st st: 24 sts and 32 rows = 4".

## ABOUT CHARTS

Read odd-numbered (RS) rows from right to left and even-numbered (WS) rows from left to right.

## BACK

With US 3, CO 149 (157, 165, 173, 181) sts.

**Foundation Row (WS):** Work Foundation Row of **Chart A** and **Chart B** as follows: k1; work sts 14-1 (10-1, 14-1, 10-1, 14-1) of **Chart B**; ([work sts 19-1 of **Chart A**; work sts 6-1 (10-1, 10-1, 14-1, 14-1) of **Chart B** ] 4 times); work sts 19-1 of **Chart A**; work sts 14-1 (10-1, 14-1, 10-1, 14-1) of **Chart B**; k1.

**Row 1 (RS):** Work Row 1 of **Chart A** and **Chart B** as follows: p1; work sts 1-14 (1-10, 1-14, 1-10, 1-14) of **Chart B**; ([work sts 1-19 of **Chart A**; work sts 1-6, (1-10, 1-10, 1-14, 1-14) of **Chart B**] 4 times); work sts 1-19 of **Chart A**; work sts 1-14 (1-10, 1-14, 1-10, 1-14) of Chart B; p1.

Continuing as set, work through Row 28 of **Chart A** and **Chart B**. Change to US 5.

**Next Row (RS):** K15 (11, 15, 11, 15); ([continue **Chart A** as set; k6 (10, 10, 14, 14)] 4 times); continue **Chart A** as set; k15 (11, 15, 11, 15).

**Next Row (WS):** P15 (11, 15, 11, 15); ([continue **Chart A** as set; p6 (10, 10, 14, 14] 4 times); continue **Chart A** as set; p15 (11, 15, 11, 15).

Continue working **Chart A** and st st as set until piece measures approx. 12½ (12½, 12½, 12½, 12½)" from CO edge, ending after working Row 17 of **Chart A**.

### INCREASE FOR AND BEGIN YOKE

**Next Row (WS): 1st Size:** P15; continue **Chart A** as set; p6; ([continue **Chart A** as set; p1, m1, p1, m1, p2, m1, p1, m1, p1] twice); continue **Chart A** as set; p6; continue **Chart A** as set; p15 (157 sts on needle).

**2nd Size:** P11; continue **Chart A** as set; p10; ([continue **Chart A** as set; p2, m1, p2, m1, p2, m1, p2, m1, p2]

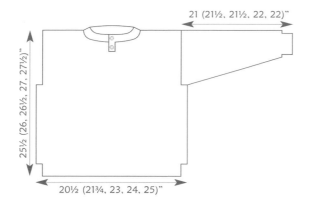

21 (21½, 21½, 22, 22)"

25½ (26, 26½, 27, 27½)"

20½ (21¾, 23, 24, 25)"

twice); continue **Chart A** as set; p10; continue **Chart A** as set; p11 (165 sts on needle).

**3rd Size:** P15; continue **Chart A** as set; p10; ([continue **Chart A** as set; p2, m1, p2, m1, p2, m1, p2, m1, p2] twice); continue **Chart A** as set; p10; continue **Chart A** as set; p15 (173 sts on needle).

**4th Size:** P11; continue **Chart A** as set; p14; ([continue **Chart A** as set; p3, m1, p2, m1, p4, m1, p2, m1, p3] twice); continue **Chart A** as set; p14; continue **Chart A** as set; p11 (181 sts on needle).

**5th Size:** P15; continue **Chart A** as set; p14; ([continue **Chart A** as set; p3, m1, p2, m1, p4, m1, p2, m1, p3] twice); continue **Chart A** as set; p14; continue **Chart A** as set; p15 (189 sts on needle).

Continuing on Row 19 of **Chart A** as set, and also beg on Row 19 of **Chart B**, set up yoke as follows:

**Next Row (RS):** K15 (11, 15, 11, 15); continue **Chart A** as set; work sts 1-6 (1-10, 1-10, 1-14, 1-14) of **Chart B**; ([continue **Chart A** as set; work sts 1-10 (1-14, 1-14, 1-18, 1-18) of **Chart B**] twice); continue **Chart A** as set; work sts 1-6 (1-10, 1-10, 1-14, 1-14) of **Chart B**; continue Chart A as set; K15 (11, 15, 11, 15).

Continue working **Chart A** and **Chart B** as set, and st st at edges, until piece measures 15 (15½, 16, 16½, 17)" from CO edge, ending with RS facing for next row.

### SHAPE ARMHOLES
BO 11 (11, 11, 11, 11) sts at beg of next 2 rows. Continue as set on rem 135 (143, 151, 159, 167) sts until piece measures 25 (25½, 26, 26½, 27)" from CO edge, ending with RS facing for next row.

### SHAPE BACK NECK
**Next Row (RS):** Work 42 (46, 50, 54, 58) sts; k2tog; place next 47 (47, 47, 47, 47) sts onto holder for back neck; place next 44 (48, 52, 56, 60) sts onto another holder for left back shoulder. Turn, and shape right back neck as follows:

**Next Row (WS):** P2tog; work to end of row.
**Next Row (RS):** Work to last 2 sts; k2tog.
**Next Row (WS):** P2tog; work to end of row.

Place rem 40 (44, 48, 52, 56) sts onto holder for right back shoulder. Break yarn.

Place sts on holder for left back shoulder onto needle, and shape left back neck as follows:

**Next Row (RS):** K2tog; work to end of row.
**Next Row (WS):** Work to last 2 sts; p2tog.
**Next Row (RS):** K2tog; work to end of row.
**Next Row (WS):** Work to last 2 sts; p2tog.

Break yarn and place rem 40 (44, 48, 52, 56) sts on holder for left back shoulder.

### FRONT
Work same as for back until piece measures 20½ (21, 21½, 22, 22½)" from CO edge, ending with RS facing for next row.

### SHAPE NECK AND PLACKET
**Next Row (RS):** Work 62 (66, 70, 74, 78) sts and place these onto holder for left front; work next 11 (11, 11, 11, 11) sts and place these onto another holder for placket.

### WORK RIGHT FRONT ONLY
Work rem 62 (66, 70, 74, 78) sts, then work 10 more rows, ending with WS facing for next row.

**Next Row (WS):** Work 54 (58, 62, 66, 70) sts; place last 8 (8, 8, 8, 8) sts on holder for front neck.

Dec 1 st at neck edge on next 14 rows. Continue without further shaping on rem (40 (44, 48, 52, 56) sts until piece measures 25½ (26, 26½, 27, 27½)" from CO edge, ending with RS facing for next row. Break yarn and place sts on holder for right front shoulder.

### WORK LEFT FRONT ONLY
Place 62 (66, 70, 74, 78) sts from holder for left front onto needle and work 9 more rows, ending with RS facing for next row.

**Next Row (RS):** Work 54 (58, 62, 66, 70) sts; place next 8 (8, 8, 8, 8) sts on holder for front neck.
**Next Row (WS):** Work to end of row.

Dec 1 st at neck edge on next 14 rows. Continue without further shaping on rem 40 (44, 48, 52, 56) sts until piece measures 25½ (26, 26½, 27, 27½)" from CO edge, ending with RS facing for next row. Break yarn and place sts on holder for left front shoulder.

## PLACKET (FOR WOMEN)

**Editor's Note:** In the following placket and neckband instructions, "cable 2" means: *slip 1 st to cn and hold at back; k1; k1 from cn.*

### RIGHT BAND

With WS facing, place 11 (11, 11, 11, 11) placket sts from holder onto US 3. Leaving a 1' tail to attach band:

**Rows 1, 3, 5 & 9 (WS):** K1, p2, k2, p1, k2, p2, k1.
**Rows 2 & 10 (RS):** P1, k2, p2, k1tbl, p2, k2, p1.
**Rows 4 & 8 (RS):** P1, cable 2, p2, k1tbl, p2, cable 2, p1.
**Row 6 (RS) (Buttonhole Row):** P1, cable 2, p1, k2, pass the knit st over the knit st, k1, pass the knit st over the knit st, k1, pass the knit st over the knit st, cable 2, p1.
**Row 7 (WS):** K1, p2, k1, CO 3, k1, p2, k1.

Don't break yarn. Using tail, attach to right front.

### LEFT BAND

With RS facing and US 3, leaving a 1' tail to attach band, pick up 11 (11, 11, 11, 11) sts behind right band.

**Rows 1, 3, 5, 7 & 9 (WS):** K1, p2, k2, p1, k2, p2, k1.
**Row 2 (RS):** P1, k2, p2, k1tbl, p2, k2, p1.
**Rows 4, 6 & 8 (RS):** P1, cable 2, p2, k1tbl, p2, cable 2, p1.

Break yarn. Place sts on holder. Using tail, attach to left front.

## PLACKET (FOR MEN)
### LEFT BAND

With RS facing, place 11 (11, 11, 11, 11) placket sts from holder onto US 3. Leaving a 1' tail to attach band:

**Rows 1 & 9 (RS):** P1, k2, p2, k1tbl, p2, k2, p1.
**Rows 2, 4, 8 & 10 (WS):** K1, p2, k2, p1, k2, p2, k1.
**Rows 3 & 7 (RS):** P1, cable 2, p2, k1tbl, p2, cable 2, p1.
**Row 5 (RS) (Buttonhole Row):** P1, cable 2, p1, k2, pass the knit st over the knit st, k1, pass the knit st over the knit st, k1, pass the knit st over the knit st, cable 2, p1.
**Row 6 (WS):** K1, p2, k1, CO 3, k1, p2, k1.

Break yarn. Place sts on holder. Using tail, attach to left front.

### RIGHT BAND

With WS facing and US 3, leaving a 1' tail, pick up 11 (11, 11, 11, 11) sts behind left band.

**Rows 1 & 9 (RS):** P1, k2, p2, k1tbl, p2, k2, p1.
**Rows 2, 4, 6 & 8 (WS):** K1, p2, k2, p1, k2, p2, k1.

**Rows 3, 5 & 7 (RS):** P1, cable 2, p2, k1tbl, p2, cable 2, p1.

Don't break yarn; continue with it to make the neckband. Place sts on holder. Use tail to attach placket to right front.

## JOIN SHOULDERS

With RS's facing, join shoulders using 3-needle bind-off method.

## NECKBAND

Place 11 (11, 11, 11, 11) sts from holder for right band onto US 3; using attached yarn, work 8 (8, 8, 8, 8) sts from holder as set; pick up 32 (32, 32, 32, 32) sts up right neck edge; place 47 (47, 47, 47, 47) sts on holder for back neck onto needle and work as follows: ([k2, p2] 4 times), k1tbl, p2, k2, p2, k1tbl, p2, k2, p2, k1tbl, ([p2, k2] 4 times); pick up 32 (32, 32, 32, 32) sts down left neck edge; work 8 (8, 8, 8, 8) sts as set; work 11 (11, 11, 11, 11) left band sts as set (149 (149, 149, 149, 149) sts on needle).

**Rows 2, 4, 6, 8, 10 & 12 (WS):** K1, p2, k2, p1, k2, p2, k2, p1, ([k2, p2] 13 times), k2, p1, ([k2, p2, k2, p1] twice), ([k2, p2] 13 times), k2, p1, k2, p2, k2, p1, k2, p2, k1.
**Rows 3 & 11 (RS):** P1, k2, p2, k1tbl, p2, k2, p2, k1tbl, ([p2, k2] 13 times), p2, k1tbl, ([p2, k2, p2, k1tbl] twice), ([p2, k2] 13 times), p2, k1tbl, p2, k2, p2, k1tbl, p2, k2, p1.
**Rows 5 & 9 (RS):** P1, cable 2, p2, k1tbl, p2, cable 2, p2, k1tbl, ([p2, cable 2] 13 times), p2, k1tbl ([p2, cable 2, p2, k1tbl] twice), ([p2, cable 2] 13 times), p2, k1tbl, p2, cable 2, p2, k1tbl, p2, cable 2, p1.
**Row 7 (RS):** Work as Row 5, making a buttonhole as in placket instructions.
**Row 8 (WS):** Work as Row 6, completing buttonhole as in placket instructions.

BO.

## SLEEVES

With US 3, CO 59 (59, 59, 59, 59) sts. Work **Foundation Row** of **Chart C**, then work Rows 1-28 of **Chart C**. Change to US 5 and rep Rows 1-28 of **Chart A** on center 19 sts and st st on all other sts, **AND AT SAME TIME**, inc 1 st at beg and end of every 4th row 15 (15, 13, 12, 10) times, then every 6th row 12 (12, 15, 16, 18) times. **ALSO AT SAME TIME**, when there are 99 (99, 97, 97, 95) sts on needle and piece measures approx. 12½ (12½, 12½, 12½, 12½)" from CO edge, ending after working Row 17 of **Chart A**:

## INCREASE FOR AND BEGIN UPPER SLEEVE PATTERN

**Next Row (WS):** P8 (8, 7, 7, 6); ([p7, m1] 4 times), p4; continue **Chart A** as set; p4, ([m1, p7] 4 times), p8 (8, 7, 7, 6).

# hjaltland pullover

Continuing Row 19 of **Chart A** as set and also beg on Row 19 of **Chart B**, set up upper sleeve as follows:

**Next Row (RS):** K8 (8, 7, 7, 6); p2; work sts 1-16 and sts 1-18 of **Chart B**; continue **Chart A** as set; work sts 1-16 and sts 1-18 of **Chart B**; p2; k8 (8, 7, 7, 6).

Continue **Chart A** and **Chart B** as set, and continue to inc as set, until there are 127 (127, 129, 129, 129) sts on needle. Work without further shaping until sleeve measures 21 (21½, 21½, 22, 22)" from CO edge, ending with RS facing for next row. BO all sts in pattern, dec'g 1 st in each small cable and 3 sts in middle cable.

## FINISHING

Sew sleeves to body. Sew side and sleeve seams. If desired, crochet a sl st edge around placket and collar. Weave in ends. Block to finished measurements. Sew on buttons opposite buttonholes.

## Chart C (Sleeve Cuff)

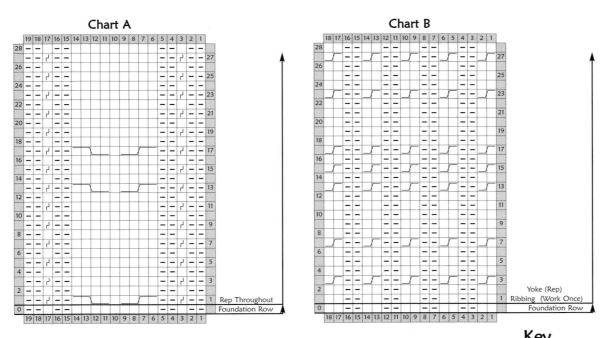

## Chart A

## Chart B

### Key

| | |
|---|---|
| ☐ | k on right side rows; p on wrong side rows. |
| − | p on right side rows; k on wrong side rows. |
| ꝋ | ktbl on right side rows; p on wrong side rows. |
| ⟋ | sl 1 st to cn and hold at back; k1; k1 from cn. |
| ⟋ | sl 2 sts to cn and hold at back; k2; k2 from cn. |
| ⟍ | sl 2 sts to cn and hold at front; k2; k2 from cn. |
| M | make 1 (inc). |
| ■ | no stitch. |

*eudora hat & scarf with hjaltland pullover*

# eudora hat

*diane brown*

---

**MATERIALS**

YARN: Jamieson's Shetland Double Knitting - 50 grams each of MC, Black (999); Color A, Sunrise (187); Color B, Old Gold (429); Color C, Mulberry (598); and Color D, Spagnum (233).

NEEDLES: 16" circular US 5 (3.75 mm) and set of double-pointed needles in same size, *or correct needle to obtain gauge.*

**MEASUREMENTS**

CIRCUMFERENCE: 21".

**GAUGE**

On US 5 in 2x2 rib: 19 sts and 28 rows = 4".

---

## SLIP STITCH PATTERN

**Rnd 1:** ([K7, sl1pwise] 15 times).
**Rnd 2:** Knit.

Rep Rnds 1-2.

## HAT

With 16" circular US 5 and MC, CO 100 sts. Place marker, join and work as follows:

**Rnd 1 (RS):** *K2, p2**; rep from * to **.

Rep the above rnd 6 times, inc'g 10 sts evenly in last rnd (110 sts on needle).

## MAKE WELT

Change to **Color A** and knit 6 rnds.

**Join Rnd:** *With right-hand needle, pick up WS st from rnd 1 of **Color A** directly below first st, place on left-hand needle, and ktog with first st**; rep from * to ** for every st in rnd.

Rep **Make Welt** instructions using **Color B**, then **Color C**, then **Color D**.

**Next Rnd:** Change to MC and knit.
**Next Rnd:** With MC, knit, inc'g 10 sts evenly around (120 sts on needle).

With MC, work in **Slip Stitch Pattern** until piece measures 5" from CO edge. Then, work dec rnds as follows, changing to double-pointed needles when sts become too stretched.

**Dec Rnd 1:** ([K6, k2tog] 15 times) (105 sts rem).
**Rnds 2, 4, 6, 8, 10, 12 & 14:** Knit.
**Dec Rnd 3:** ([K5, k2tog] 15 times) (90 sts rem).
**Dec Rnd 5:** ([K4, k2tog] 15 times) (75 sts rem).
**Dec Rnd 7:** ([K3, k2tog] 15 times) (60 sts rem).
**Dec Rnd 9:** ([K2, k2tog] 15 times) (45 sts rem).
**Dec Rnd 11:** ([K1, k2tog] 15 times) (30 sts rem).
**Dec Rnd 13:** K2tog to end of rnd (15 sts rem).
**Dec Rnd 15:** K1, ([k2tog] 7 times) (8 sts rem).

Break yarn, leaving 8" tail. Thread tapestry needle and pass through rem 8 sts. Pull tog tightly and secure on WS.

## CORDED BUTTON (OPTIONAL)

With US 5 double-pointed needle and Color A, CO 3 sts.

**Row 1:** K3; without turning, slide sts to other end of needle, pulling yarn tightly across back.

Rep Row 1 above until cord measures 3". BO. Shape cord into circle and sew to top of hat.

# eudora scarf

*gregory courtney*

---

**MATERIALS**

**YARN:** Jamieson's Shetland Double Knitting - 50 grams each of Color A, Black (999); Color B, Sunrise (187); Color C, Old Gold (429); Color D, Mulberry (598); and Color E, Spagnum (233).
**NEEDLES:** Short US 6 (4 mm) *or correct needle to obtain gauge.*

**MEASUREMENTS**
**WIDTH:** 3¾".
**LENGTH:** Approx. 100".

**GAUGE**
On US 6 in **Chart**: 21 sts and 28 rows = 4".

---

## Chart

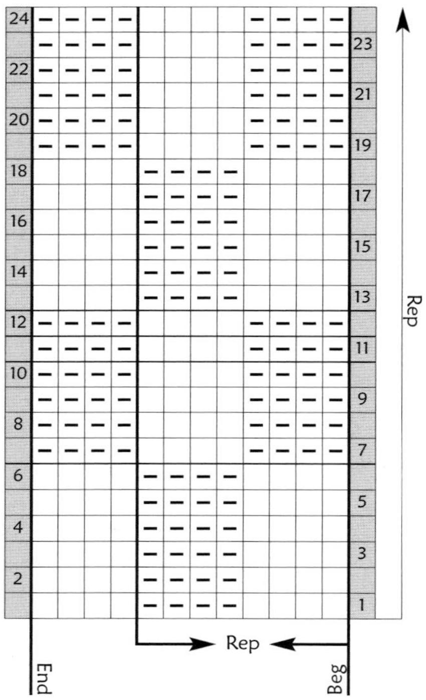

*(chart showing 24 rows, with "Rep" marked along the right side and bottom, "End" at bottom left and "Beg" at bottom right)*

## SCARF

With US 6 and Color A, CO 20 sts. Reading odd-numbered (RS) rows from right to left and even-numbered (WS) rows from left to right, *with Color A, work the 24 rows of **Chart**; with Color B, work the 24 rows of **Chart**; with Color C, work the 24 rows of **Chart**; with Color D, work the 24 rows of **Chart**; with Color E, work the 24 rows of **Chart**.** Rep from * to ** until scarf measures approx. 100" (or desired length). BO.

## FINISHING

Weave in ends. Block gently to finished measurements.

## Key

☐ k on right side rows; p on wrong side rows.
— p on right side rows; k on wrong side rows.

# Archaeology and Knitting
## THE GUNNISTER PURSE

**W**hile on a tour of the Shetland Isles last fall, I broke away from the group one gray afternoon to visit the Shetland Museum. A strong interest in archaeology and social history (and, of course, knitting) made this visit a happy prospect. Knitting is a prominent part of Shetland history; however, being such an ordinary part of everyday life there, knitted articles and knitting implements in the museum often show up unexpectedly in display cases amidst a jumble of other artifacts. If I had not been looking specifically for things concerning knitting, I might have missed the Gunnister Purse. It lies in a display case containing an assortment of artifacts, including some from a late 17th-century grave discovered in a peat bank at Gunnister, Shetland, that was excavated in 1951. The purse—a reproduction—sports three narrow Fair Isle bands, a drawstring at the top, and tassels along the bottom edge. In the purse were found a few Dutch and Swedish coins and a length of ribbon—items probably acquired from foreign traders or visiting sailors. The original purse is the oldest known piece of two-color Shetland knitting.

**I** asked a man working at the museum if he had any further information about the purse. He stepped into a back office and appeared a few minutes later carrying an old cloth-bound book about Shetland history, opened to an article about the discovery of the grave at Gunnister. Black and white photos showed the knitted and woven clothing found in the grave. The article detailed each knitted item, right down to the number of rows and repeats, and speculated as to the colors used. I photocopied the article, with the intention of recreating the purse.

**O**n the way back to the hotel, I couldn't stop thinking about the purse, so I decided to start work on it that very afternoon. Armed with my double-pointed knitting needles and some jumper-weight wool I had purchased during my visit, I began. I became preoccupied with the project, and knitted on it constantly—in my room, with friends, on the tour bus—any spare moment I could find. While knitting, I often thought of the owner of the original purse. Who was he? How did he die? Was the ribbon in his purse a gift? And if so, was it a gift received, or one to be given? One can only guess as to the identity and social status of the "Gunnister Man," but the knitted garments and purse strongly suggest that he was a native Shetlander.

**B**ack now in my studio, I look at the small knitted purse and realize how a knitter is but a link in a long chain of artisans who create items that inspire generations. Of all the things I brought back from my trip, I prize most of all that small discovery in the Shetland Museum.

TO LEARN MORE ABOUT THE GUNNISTER MAN AND SHETLAND KNITTING, VISIT THE SHETLAND MUSEUM ONLINE AT WWW.SHETLAND-MUSEUM.ORG.UK. ALL THE CLOTHING EXCAVATED AT GUNNISTER CAN BE SEEN AT THE ROYAL MUSEUM OF SCOTLAND IN EDINBURGH.

*Diane Brown*

## RIB PATTERN

**Every Rnd:** *K2, p2**; rep from * to **.

## PICOT HEM PATTERN

**Rnd 1:** *K2tog, yo**; rep from * to **.
**Rnd 2:** Knit.

## GUNNISTER PURSE

With US 1 and Pacific, CO 76 sts. Join and work 4 rnds in **Rib Pattern**; work the 2 rnds of **Picot Hem Pattern**; work 4 rnds in **Rib Pattern**. Change to Mogit and continue in **Rib Pattern** until piece measures approx. 2" from CO edge. Work 5 rnds in st st, dec'g 4 sts evenly in last rnd (72 sts).

Work **Chart A**, then change to Mogit and work 10 rnds in st st. Work **Chart B**, then change to Mogit and work 10 rnds in st st. Work **Chart C**, then change to Mogit and work 5 rnds in st st. Place 36 sts each on separate holders, with beg of rnd at one end of holder.

## BRAIDED CORD

Cut nine 24" strands (5 of Mogit, 2 each of Copper and Pacific). Divide into 3 sets of 3 strands each and braid tog.

## TASSELS (MAKE 3)

Cut piece of cardboard 3" wide by length desired for tassel. Wrap each yarn color 3-4 times around length of cardboard. Cut another length of Mogit about 12" long and tie strands tog at upper edge of cardboard. Cut yarn at lower edge. Tie tassel together with another piece of Mogit approx. ¼" below top knot. Trim ends.

## FINISHING

Close bottom of purse using 3-needle bind-off method or weave tog using kitchener st. Fold upper edge to inside along picot hem and sew down loosely. Thread one end of braided cord into eye of large tapestry needle, insert through eyelet at front of purse, work around hem and pull through adjacent eyelet. Adjust length and tie both ends of braid. Trim ends. Attach tassels to each corner and middle of bottom edge of purse. Weave in ends. Block lightly.

### Chart A

### Chart B

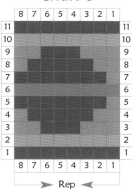

### Chart C

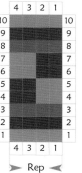

### Color Key

Copper (879)
Mogit (107)
Olive (825)
Pacific (763)
Yellow Ochre (230)

# glen orchy pullover

## gregory courtney

---

### MATERIALS

**Yarn:** Jamieson's Chunky Shetland - 800 (800, 900) grams.
Shown in Harvest (2101).
**Needles:** 16" circular US 8 (5 mm) and 32" circular US 10
(6 mm), *or correct needles to obtain gauge.*
**Accessories:** Stitch holders.

### MEASUREMENTS

**Chest:** 42 (46, 50)".
**Length to Armhole:** 14½ (15, 16)".
**Armhole Depth:** 9½ (10, 10)".
**Length:** 24 (25, 26)".
**Sleeve Length to Underarm:** 17 (18, 18)".
**Sleeve Length to Shoulder:** 20 (21, 21)".

### GAUGE

On US 10 in **Waffle Stitch:** 16 sts and 24 rows = 4".

---

### ABOUT CHARTS

Read odd-numbered (RS) rows from right to left and
even-numbered (WS) rows from left to right.

### WAFFLE STITCH (MULTIPLE OF 4+2)

**Row 1 (RS):** *K2, p2**; rep from * to **; end k2.
**Row 2 (WS):** *P2, k2**; rep from * to **; end p2.
**Row 3 (RS):** Knit.
**Row 4 (WS):** Purl.

Rep Rows 1-4.

### BACK

With US 10, CO 92 (100, 108) sts. Work **Foundation Row**
of **Chart A**, then rep Rows 1-24 of **Chart A** until piece
measures 14½ (15, 16)" from CO edge, ending after working **Row 2 of Waffle Stitch** portion of chart and with RS
and **Row 3 of Waffle Stitch** facing for next row.

### SHAPE ARMHOLES

BO 8 (8, 8) sts at beg of next 2 rows, then dec 1 st at beg
and end of every occurrence of **Row 3 of Waffle Stitch**
portion of chart 4 (4, 4) times as follows: k2, k2tog; work
to last 4 sts; ssk, k2. Work without further shaping on rem
68 (76, 84) sts until piece measures 23 (24, 25)" from CO
edge, ending with RS facing for next row.

### SHAPE NECK

**Next Row (RS):** Work 18 (22, 26) sts and place on
holder; work 32 (32, 32) sts and place on holder for back
neck; work 18 (22, 26) sts.

Turn, and working each side separately, dec 1 st at neck
edge on next 2 (2, 2) rows, then work without further
shaping on rem 16 (20, 24) sts until piece measures 24
(25, 26)" from CO edge. Place shoulder sts on holders.

### FRONT

Work same as for back until piece measures 21 (22, 23)"
from CO edge, ending with RS facing for next row.

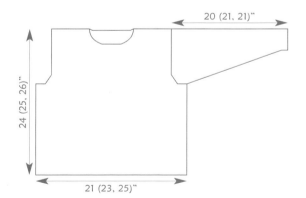

20 (21, 21)"

24 (25, 26)"

21 (23, 25)"

*glen orchy pullover (right)*

### SHAPE NECK

**NEXT ROW (RS):** Work 24 (28, 32) sts and place on holder; work 20 (20, 20) sts and place on holder for front neck; work 24 (28, 32) sts.

Turn, and working each side separately, dec 1 st at neck edge on every RS row 8 (8, 8) times. Work without further shaping on rem 16 (20, 24) sts until piece measures 24 (25, 26)" from CO edge. Place shoulder sts on holders.

### JOIN SHOULDERS

With RS's facing, join shoulders using 3-needle bind-off method.

### SLEEVES

With US 8, CO 32 (32, 32) sts. Work in garter st for 1¼ (1¼, 1¼)", ending with WS facing for next row.

**Next Row (WS):** K2 (2, 2), m1, k28 (28, 28), m1, k2 (2, 2) (34 (34, 34) sts on needle).

Change to US 10 and rep the 4 rows of **Waffle Stitch, AND AT SAME TIME,** inc 1 st at beg and end of every 4th row 15 (23, 23) times, then every 6th row 5 (1, 1) time(s) (74 (82, 82) sts on needle). Work without further shaping until piece measures 17 (18, 18)" from CO edge, ending after working **Row 2 of Waffle Stitch** and with RS and **Row 3 of Waffle Stitch** facing for next row.

### SHAPE SLEEVE CAP

BO 8 (8, 8) sts at beg of next 2 rows, then dec 1 st at beg and end of every occurrence of **Row 3 of Waffle Stitch** 4 (4, 4) times as follows: k2, k2tog; work to last 4 sts; ssk, k2. After last dec row, BO rem 50 (58, 58) sts.

### NECKBAND

With US 8, RS facing, beg at right shoulder seam, pick up 6 (6, 6) sts from shoulder seam to back neck holder; k32 (32, 32) sts from back neck holder, dec'g 8 (8, 8) sts evenly spaced across (24 (24, 24) sts rem); pick up 6 (6, 6) sts to left shoulder seam; pick up 21 (21, 21) sts down left neck edge; k20 (20, 20) sts from front neck holder, dec'g 8 (8, 8) sts evenly spaced across (12 (12, 12) sts rem); pick up 21 (21, 21) sts up right neck edge (90 (90, 90) sts on needle). Work in garter st until neckband measures 1¼ (1¼, 1¼)". BO.

### FINISHING

Sew sleeves to body. Sew side and sleeve seams. Weave in ends. Block to finished measurements.

## Chart A (Front and Back)

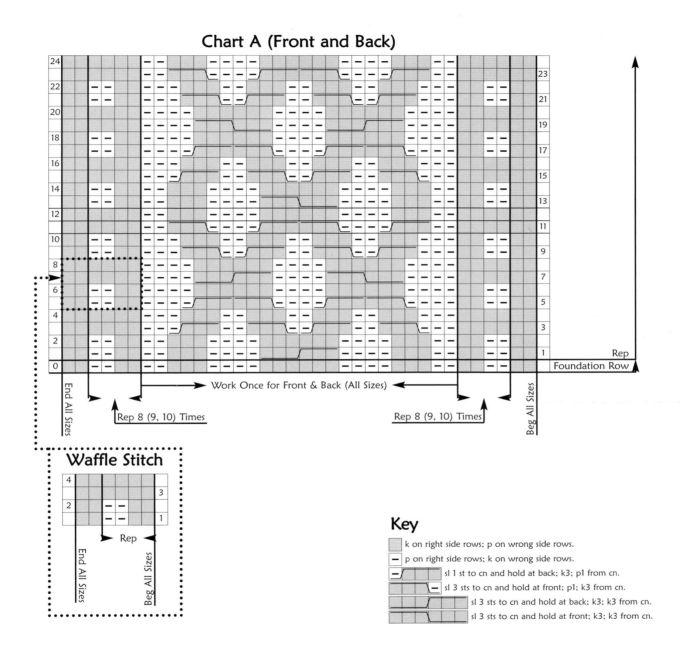

Work Once for Front & Back (All Sizes)

Rep 8 (9, 10) Times

Rep 8 (9, 10) Times

End All Sizes

Beg All Sizes

Rep

Foundation Row

### Waffle Stitch

End All Sizes

Beg All Sizes

Rep

### Key

k on right side rows; p on wrong side rows.

— p on right side rows; k on wrong side rows.

sl 1 st to cn and hold at back; k3; p1 from cn.

sl 3 sts to cn and hold at front; p1; k3 from cn.

sl 3 sts to cn and hold at back; k3; k3 from cn.

sl 3 sts to cn and hold at front; k3; k3 from cn.

# jazz pullover

## louise irvine

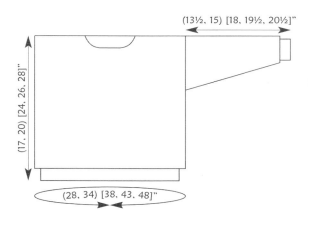

<table>
<tr><td></td><td>(13½, 15) [18, 19½, 20½]"</td></tr>
</table>

(13½, 15) [18, 19½, 20½]"

(17, 20) [24, 26, 28]"

(28, 34) [38, 43, 48]"

---

<table>
<thead>
<tr><th>MATERIALS</th></tr>
</thead>
</table>

**MATERIALS**
(CHILDREN'S AMOUNTS IN PARENTHESES)
[ADULT'S AMOUNTS IN BRACKETS]
YARN: Jamieson's Shetland 2-Ply Spindrift - (50, 50) [75, 75, 75] grams of Mogit (107); (50, 50) [50, 75, 75] grams of Royal (700); (25, 25) [50, 50, 50] grams of Amber (478); (25, 25) [25, 50, 50] grams of Caspian (760); (25, 50) [50, 50, 50] grams of Copper (879); (25, 50) [50, 50, 75] grams of Daffodil (390); (25, 25) [50, 50, 75] grams of Grouse (235); (25, 25) [50, 50, 75] grams of Ivy (815); (50, 50) [50, 75, 75] grams of Lemon (350); (25, 25) [25, 50, 50] grams of Madder (587); (25, 25) [25, 25, 25] grams of Mint (770); and (25, 25) [25, 25, 25] grams of Sandalwood (861).
NEEDLES: Circular and/or double-pointed US 2 (3 mm) and US 3 (3.25 mm), *or correct needles to obtain gauge.*
ACCESSORIES: Stitch holders. Tapestry needle (for finishing).

**MEASUREMENTS**
(CHILDREN'S SIZES IN PARENTHESES)
[ADULT'S SIZES IN BRACKETS]
CHEST: (29, 34) [38, 43, 48]".
LENGTH TO ARMHOLE: (10, 12) [15, 16½, 18]".
ARMHOLE DEPTH: (7, 8) [9, 9½, 10]".
LENGTH: (17, 20) [24, 26, 28]".
SLEEVE LENGTH: (13½, 15) [18, 19½, 20½]".

**GAUGE**
On US 3 in **Chart**: 30 sts and 30 rows = 4".

---

## ABOUT CHARTS
As garment is knit entirely in the rnd, read all rows from right to left. Knit all sts in **Chart**.

## BODY
With US 2 and Mogit, CO (196, 228) [260, 292, 320] sts. Place marker, join and work in the rnd as follows:

**Rnds 1 & 2:** *With Mogit, k2, p2**; rep from * to **.
**Rnd 3:** *K2 Royal, p2 Mogit**; rep from * to **.

Rep Rnd 3 until piece measures (1¾, 2) [2, 2½, 2½]" from CO edge. Change to Mogit and work in st st for 2 rnds, inc'g on 2nd rnd for your size as follows:

**1st Children's Size:** m1, k6; ([m1, k10] 19 times) (216 sts on needle). **2nd Children's Size:** K12; ([m1, k9] 24 times) (252 sts on needle). **1st Adult's Size:** K8; ([m1, k9] 28 times) (288 sts on needle). **2nd Adult's Size:** K4; ([m1, k9] 32 times) (324 sts on needle). **3rd Adult's Size:** ([m1, k8] 40 times) (360 sts on needle).

Change to US 3 and beg and ending at points marked for your size, work **Foundation Row** of **Chart** once, then rep **Chart** until (65, 79) [103, 111, 123] rnds have been worked.

# jazz pullover

### SET ARMHOLE STEEKS

**Next Rnd:** Place 1st st of rnd on holder. With alt colors, CO 5 sts (1 edge st and 4 steek sts); mark 1st cast-on st for beg of rnd; continue **Chart** as set on next (107, 125) [143, 161, 179] sts; place next st on holder; CO 10 sts (1 edge st on each side and 8 steek sts); continue **Chart** as set on next (107, 125) [143, 161, 179] sts; with alt colors, CO 5 sts (1 edge st and 4 steek sts).

Working steek sts in alt colors and edge sts in background color, continue **Chart** as set for (35, 42) [50, 54, 58] more rnds.

### SHAPE NECK

**Next Rnd:** Work 4 steek sts and 1 edge st; continue **Chart** as set on next (45, 52) [58, 65, 72] sts; place next (17, 21) [27, 31, 35] sts on holder for front neck. With alt colors, CO 8 steek sts; continue **Chart** to end of rnd.

Continuing **Chart** as set, dec 1 st at each side of neck steek on next 6 rnds, then every alt rnd (3, 4) [5, 5, 5] times ((36, 42) [47, 54, 61] sts rem for each shoulder). Work (8, 8) [6, 6, 6] more rnds. On following rnd, BO all steek sts. Place (35, 41) [49, 53, 57] back neck sts on holder.

### JOIN SHOULDERS

With Mogit, join shoulders using 3-needle bind-off method (or weave with kitchener st, if desired).

### SLEEVES

Cut sleeve steeks open through center st (between 4th and 5th sts) and back stitch up center of 1st and last steek sts.

Place st from holder onto US 3 circular or double-pointed needle and mark this st as beg of rnd. With Mogit, pick up (108, 116) [128, 136, 144] sts between edge st and steek st evenly around armhole. Turning **Chart** upside down and

working backwards through chart, beg and ending at points marked for your size, and working the marked st in background color throughout, work Rows (97-93, 4-2 & 97-96) [27-23, 36-32, 43-39]. Then, continue backwards through chart, **AND AT SAME TIME**, dec 1 st on each side of marked st every 4th rnd (14, 16) [27, 30, 25] times, then every 3rd rnd (12, 12) [5, 4, 13] times ((57, 61) [65, 69, 69] sts rem).

### DEC FOR CUFF

**Next Rnd:** With Mogit, work in st st, dec'g (1, 1) [1, 1, 1] st. Change to US 2 and work as follows:

**Next Rnd:** *K2 Royal, p2 Mogit**; rep from * to **.

Rep this rnd until cuff measures (1¾, 2) [2, 2½, 2½]", then work above rnd with Mogit only for 2 more rnds. With Mogit, BO.

### FINISHING

Secure 1st and last st of front neck steek. Cut steek through center st.

### NECKBAND

With US 2 and Mogit, knit the (35, 41) [49, 53, 57] sts from back neck holder; pick up (26, 27) [28, 30, 32] sts down left front neck edge; knit the (17, 21) [27, 31, 35] sts from front neck holder; pick up (26, 27) [28, 30, 32] up right front neck edge ((104, 116) [132, 144, 156] sts on needle).

**Next Rnd:** *K2 Royal, p2 Mogit**; rep from * to **.

Rep this rnd until neck measures (1, 1) [1½, 1½, 1½]", then work above rnd with Mogit only for 2 more rnds. With Mogit, BO.

Trim all steeks and cross stitch in place. Weave in ends. Block to finished measurements.

# jazz pullover

## Chart

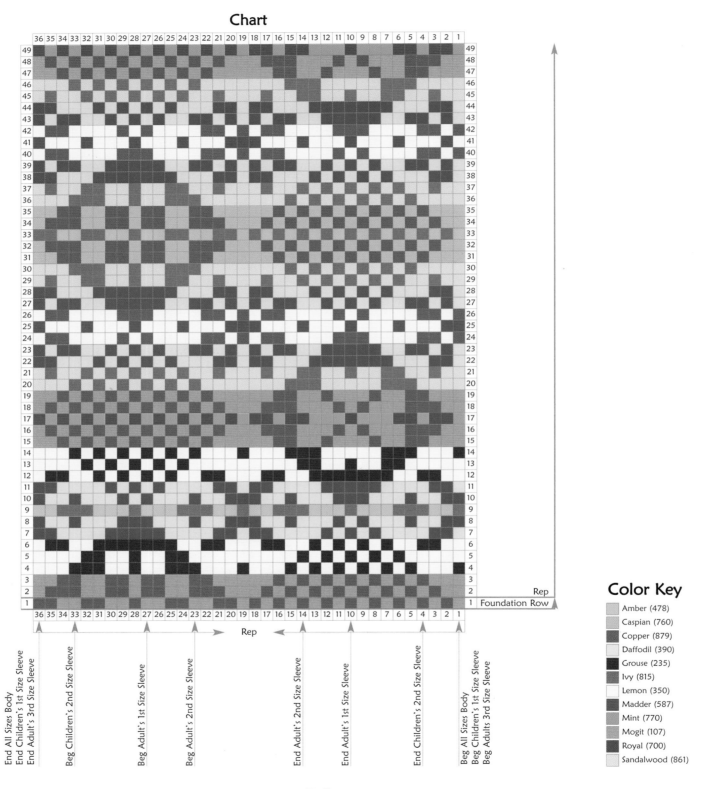

### Color Key

| | |
|---|---|
| | Amber (478) |
| | Caspian (760) |
| | Copper (879) |
| | Daffodil (390) |
| | Grouse (235) |
| | Ivy (815) |
| | Lemon (350) |
| | Madder (587) |
| | Mint (770) |
| | Mogit (107) |
| | Royal (700) |
| | Sandalwood (861) |

## Chart (Cont'd)

Rep (Cont'd)

Rep

## Color Key

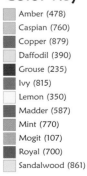

- Amber (478)
- Caspian (760)
- Copper (879)
- Daffodil (390)
- Grouse (235)
- Ivy (815)
- Lemon (350)
- Madder (587)
- Mint (770)
- Mogit (107)
- Royal (700)
- Sandalwood (861)

# prince caspian pullover

*diane brown*

---

## MATERIALS

**YARN:** Jamieson's Shetland Double Knitting - 200 (250, 300) grams. Shown in Amber (478).

**NEEDLES:** 16" and 32" circular US 5 (3.75 mm) and 32" circular US 6 (4 mm), *or correct needles to obtain gauge.*

**ACCESSORIES:** Cable needle. Stitch holders.

## MEASUREMENTS

**CHEST:** 27 (32, 36)".
**LENGTH TO ARMHOLE:** 10 (11½, 14½)".
**ARMHOLE DEPTH:** 7 (7½, 8½)".
**LENGTH:** 17 (19, 23)".
**SLEEVE LENGTH:** 13 (14, 17)".

## GAUGE

On US 5 in **False Rib Pattern**: 22 sts and 32 rows = 4".

---

## ABOUT CHARTS

Read odd-numbered (RS) rows from right to left and even-numbered (WS) rows from left to right.

## FALSE RIB PATTERN (OVER ODD NO. OF STS)

**Row 1 (RS):** *K1, p1**; rep from * to ** to last st; k1.
**Row 2 (WS):** Knit.

Rep Rows 1-2.

## BACK

With US 6, CO 74 (86, 98) sts. Work 4 rows in garter st, ending with RS facing for next row:

**Row 1 (RS):** *K2, p2**; rep from * to ** to last 2 sts; k2.
**Row 2 (WS):** *P2, k2**; rep from * to ** to last 2 sts; p2.

Work these 2 rows rows twice more.

Work first separation welt as follows:

**Row 1 (RS):** Knit, dec'g 5 (3, 1) sts evenly across row (69 (83, 97) sts on needle).
**Rows 2 & 6 (WS):** Knit.
**Rows 3 & 5 (RS):** Purl.
**Row 4 (WS)** Purl.

Change to US 5 and work the 20 rows of **Chart**, ending with RS facing for next row. **Note:** St count has inc'd by 2 sts upon completion of **Chart** (71 (85, 99) sts on needle).

Work second separation welt as follows:

**Rows 1 & 5 (RS):** Knit.
**Row 2 (WS):** Purl.
**Row 3 (RS):** Purl.
**Row 4 (WS):** Knit.
**Row 6 (WS):** Knit, inc'g 10 (6, 6) sts evenly across row (81 (91, 105) sts on needle).

Work in **False Rib Pattern** until piece measures 16 (18, 22)" from CO edge, ending with RS facing for next row.

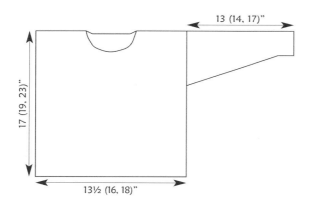

13 (14, 17)"

17 (19, 23)"

13½ (16, 18)"

*prince caspian pullover (front)*

### SHAPE BACK NECK
**NEXT ROW (RS):** Work 27 (32, 36) sts; BO 27 (27, 33) sts for back neck; work 27 (32, 36) sts.

Turn, and working each side separately, BO 2 (2, 2) sts at neck edge 1 (1, 1) time, then 1 (1, 1) st 1 (2, 2) time(s). Work without further shaping on rem 24 (28, 32) sts until piece measures 17 (19, 23)" from CO edge, ending after working a RS row. Place shoulder sts on holders.

### FRONT
Work same as for back until piece measures 14 (16, 20)" from CO edge, ending with RS facing for next row.

### SHAPE FRONT NECK
**Next Row (RS):** Work 29 (33, 37) sts; BO 23 (25, 31) sts for front neck; work 29 (33, 37) sts.

Turn, and working each side separately, BO 2 (2, 2) sts at neck edge 2 (1, 1) time(s), then 1 (1, 1) st 1 (3, 3) time(s). Work without further shaping on rem 24 (28, 32) sts until piece measures same as back. Place shoulder sts on holders.

### JOIN SHOULDERS
With RS's facing, join shoulders using 3-needle bind-off method.

### SLEEVES
With US 6, CO 46 (46, 58) sts. Work 4 rows in garter st, ending with RS facing for next row:

**Row 1 (RS):** *K2, p2**; rep from * to ** to last 2 sts; k2.
**Row 2 (WS):** *P2, k2**; rep from * to ** to last 2 sts; p2.

Work these 2 rows rows twice more.

Work first separation welt as follows:

**Row 1 (RS):** Knit to end, dec'g 5 (5, 3) sts evenly across row (41 (41, 55) sts on needle).
**Rows 2 & 6 (WS):** Knit.
**Rows 3 & 5 (RS):** Purl.
**Row 4 (WS)** Purl.

Change to US 5 and work the 20 rows of **Chart**, ending with RS facing for next row. **Note:** St count has inc'd by 2 sts upon completion of **Chart** (43 (43, 57) sts on needle).

Work second separation welt as follows:

**Rows 1 & 5 (RS):** Knit.
**Row 2 (WS):** Purl.
**Row 3 (RS):** Purl.
**Row 4 (WS):** Knit.
**Row 6 (WS):** Knit, inc'g 4 (6, 8) sts evenly across row (47 (49, 65) sts on needle).

Work in **False Rib Pattern, AND AT SAME TIME,** on WS rows, inc 1 st at beg and end of every 4th row 13 (15, 10) times, then every 6th row 0 (0, 7) times (73 (79, 99) sts on needle). Work without further shaping until piece measures 13 (14, 17)" from CO edge, ending with RS facing for next row. BO all sts.

### NECKBAND
With US 5, RS facing, beg at left shoulder, pick up 17 (17, 18) sts down left neck edge, 23 (25, 29) sts along front neck edge, 17 (17, 18) sts up right neck edge; and 35 (39, 43) sts along back neck edge (92 (98, 108) sts on needle).

Join, and work welt as follows:

**Next Rnd:** Knit.
**Next Rnd:** Purl.
**Next Rnd:** Purl.
**Next Rnd:** Knit, dec'g 4 (6, 4) sts evenly across row (88 (92, 104) sts on needle).

**Rnd 1 (RS):** *K2, p2**; rep from * to **.

Work this rnd 3 (4, 5) more times.

Work 4 rnds in garter st. BO loosely.

### FINISHING
Center sleeves on shoulder seams and sew into place. Sew sleeve and side seams. Weave in ends. Block lightly to finished measurements.

## Chart

Rep 4 (5, 6) Times Body
Rep 2 (2, 3) Times Sleeves

End All Sizes

Beg All Sizes

NOTE: AT COMPLETION OF CHART, ST COUNT HAS INC'D BY 2 STS FOR ALL SIZES.

## Key

☐ k on right side rows; p on wrong side rows.

— p on right side rows; k on wrong side rows.

╱ k2tog.

╲ ssk.

⩔ k into back and front of st; pick up and k vertical thread btwn 2 sts just worked (double inc on RS).

⩔ p and leave on needle; yo; p into same st (double inc on WS).

B make bobble: k into back, front and back of st; turn; p3; turn; k3; turn; p3; turn; sl1, k2tog, psso.

⚠ sl next 3 sts, one-at-a-time, onto right-hand needle; pass 2nd st over 1st st; return this st to left-hand needle; pass 2nd st over this st; pass this st back to right-hand needle; pass 2nd st over this st; pass this st back to left-hand needle; pass 2nd st over this st; purl this st.

sl 1st to cn and hold at back; k2; k1 from cn.

sl 2 sts to cn and hold at front; k1; k2 from cn.

sl 1st to cn and hold at back; k2; p1 from cn.

sl 2 sts to cn and hold at front; p1; k2 from cn.

■ no stitch.

# sand lodge pullover

*wilma malcombson*

## MATERIALS

**YARN:** Jamieson's Shetland 2-Ply Spindrift - 75 (75, 100) grams of Bramble (155); 75 (75, 100) grams of Dusk (165); 75 (100, 100) grams of Mogit (107); 75 (75, 100) grams of Moorgrass (286); 75 (100, 100) grams of Pacific (763); 75 (75, 75) grams of Olive (825); and 25 (50, 50) of grams Yellow Ochre (230).

**NEEDLES:** Circular and/or double-pointed US 2 (3 mm) and US 3 (3.25 mm), *or correct needles to obtain gauge.*

**ACCESSORIES:** Stitch holders. Tapestry needle (for finishing).

## MEASUREMENTS

CHEST: 42 (48, 54)".
LENGTH TO ARMHOLE: 15 (16½, 16½)".
ARMHOLE DEPTH: 9 (10, 11)".
LENGTH: 24 (26½, 27½)".
SLEEVE LENGTH: 19½ (20½, 21½)".

## GAUGE

On US 3 in **Chart B**: 32 sts and 32 rows = 4".

## ABOUT CHARTS

As garment is knit entirely in the rnd, read all rows from right to left. Work **Chart A** and **Chart C** in p2, k2 (corrugated) rib. Knit all sts in **Chart B**.

## BODY

With US 2 and Olive, CO 284 (324, 368) sts. Place marker, join and work the 18 rows of **Chart A**.

**Next Rnd:** Change to US 3 and with Dusk, knit, inc'g as follows: **1st Size:** k2; ([m1, k10] 28 times); end k2 (312 sts on needle). **2nd Size:** ([m1, k9] 36 times) (360 sts on needle). **3rd Size:** k4; ([m1, k9] 40 times); end k4 (408 sts on needle).

Beg and ending at points marked for your size, rep **Chart B** until 103 (115, 115) rnds have been worked.

## SET ARMHOLE STEEKS

**Next Rnd:** Place 1st st of rnd on holder. With alt colors, CO 5 sts (1 edge st and 4 steek sts); mark 1st cast-on st for beg of rnd; continue **Chart B** as set on next 155 (179, 203) sts; place next st on holder; CO 10 sts (1 edge st on each side and 8 steek sts); continue **Chart B** as set on next 155 (179, 203) sts; with alt colors, CO 5 sts (1 edge st and 4 steek sts).

Working steek sts in alt colors and edge sts in background color, continue **Chart B** as set for 15 (17, 17) more rnds.

## SHAPE NECK

**Next Rnd:** Work 4 steek sts and 1 edge st; continue **Chart B** as set on next 77 (89, 101) sts, placing center st on holder for neckband. With alt colors, CO 8 steek sts; continue **Chart B** to end of rnd.

Continuing **Chart B** as set, dec 1 st at each side of neck steek every 2nd rnd 26 (30, 34) times. Work rem 51 (59, 67) sts for 6 (4, 2) more rnds. On following rnd, BO all steek sts. Place 49 (61, 69) back neck sts on holder.

## JOIN SHOULDERS

With Dusk, join shoulders using 3-needle bind-off method (or weave with kitchener st, if desired).

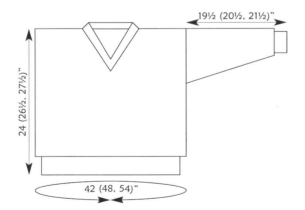

19½ (20½, 21½)"

24 (26½, 27½)"

42 (48, 54)"

backwards through chart, beg and ending at points marked for your size, and working the marked st in background color through-out, work Rows 38-34 (38-34, 38-34). Then, continue backwards through chart, **AND AT SAME TIME**, dec 1 st on each side of marked st every 4th rnd 36 (38, 43) times (73 (81, 83) sts rem).

### DEC FOR CUFF

**Next Rnd:** With Dusk, work in st st, dec'g as follows: **1st Size:** K5; ([k2tog, k13] 5 times); end k2tog, k6 (68 sts on needle). **2nd Size:** ([K7, k2tog] 9 times) (72 sts on needle). **3rd Size:** K8, k2tog; ([k5, k2tog] 9 times); end k8, k2tog (72 sts on needle).

Work the 18 rows of **Chart A** once. With Olive, BO.

### FINISHING

Secure 1st and last st of front neck steek. Cut steek through center st.

### NECKBAND

With US 3 and Olive, pick up 81 (87, 91) sts up right front neck edge; knit the 49 (61, 69) sts from back neck holder, pick up 80 (86, 90) sts down left front neck edge; knit the st on holder at center front (211, (235, 251) sts on needle). Join, mark beg of rnd, and work the 11 rows of **Chart C** as follows:

**Rnd 1:** *K2, p2**; rep from * to ** to last 3 sts; k1, sl1, k2tog (last st of current rnd and 1st st of next rnd), psso.
**Rnd 2:** K1, *p2, k2**; rep from * to ** to last 4 sts; p2, sl1, k2tog (last st of current rnd and 1st st of next rnd), psso.
**Rnd 3:** *P2, k2**; rep from * to ** to last 3 sts; p1, sl1, k2tog (last st of current rnd and 1st st of next rnd), psso.
**Rnd 4:** P1, *k2, p2**; rep from * to ** to last 4 sts; k2, sl1, k2tog (last st of current rnd and 1st st of next rnd), psso.

### SLEEVES

Cut sleeve steeks open through center st (between 4th and 5th sts) and back stitch up center of 1st and last steek sts.

Place st from holder onto US 3 circular or double-pointed needle and mark this st as beg of rnd. With Dusk, pick up 144 (156, 168) sts between edge st and steek st evenly around armhole. Turning **Chart B** upside down and working

Rep these 4 rnds once more, then work Rnds 1-3 once more. With Olive, BO.

Trim all steeks and cross stitch in place. Weave in ends. Block to finished measurements.

## Chart B

## Chart A

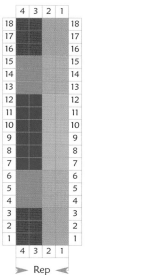

**Note on Charts A & C:**
With color indicated,
purl sts 1-2 and knit sts
3-4.

## Chart C

Rep

## Color Key

- Bramble (155)
- Dusk (165)
- Mogit (107)
- Moorgrass (286)
- Olive (825)
- Pacific (763)
- Yellow Ochre (230)

# barclay scarf

*gregory courtney*

## MATERIALS

YARN: Jamieson's Soft Shetland - 100 (100) grams each of Color A, Color B, and Color C. Nate wears the 8½" x 60" unfringed version on the opposite page in Color A, Grouse (1090); Color B, Pine (234); and Color C, Purple Heather (239). Gabrielle wears the 5" x 90" fringed version on page 57 in Color A, Midnight (1340); Color B, Amethyst (1310); and Color C, Purple Heather (239).
NEEDLES: US 6 (4 mm), *or correct needle to obtain gauge.*

## MEASUREMENTS

WIDTH: 5 (8½)".
LENGTH: 90 (60)" (excluding fringe).

## GAUGE

On US 6 in **3-Color Box Stitch**: 18 sts and 32 rows = 4".

## 3-COLOR BOX STITCH (MULTIPLE OF 4 + 2)

**Row 1 (RS):** With Color A, *k2, p2**; rep from * to **; end k2.

**Row 2 (WS):** With Color B, *k2, p2**; rep from * to **; end k2.

**Row 3 (RS):** With Color C, *k2, p2**; rep from * to **; end k2.

**Row 4 (WS):** With Color A, *k2, p2**; rep from * to **; end k2.

**Row 5 (RS):** With Color B, *k2, p2**; rep from * to **; end k2.

**Row 6 (WS):** With Color C, *k2, p2**; rep from * to **; end k2.

Rep Rows 1-6.

## DESIGNER NOTES

Even though WS and RS rows are given, the pattern looks the same on both sides. Carry unused colors along edges, holding unused strand behind new strand at beg of row. This will make an attractive "corded" edge.

## SCARF

With US 6 and Color A, CO 22 (38) sts.

Work Rows 2-6 of **3-Color Box Stitch**, then rep Rows 1-6 until piece measures approx. 90 (60)". BO in knit on a Color A row.

## FINISHING

Weave in ends carefully, matching "corded" edge as closely as possible. Block to finished measurements. Attach fringe, if desired.

# Burra Bears

They appear everywhere in Shetland. They peer at you quizzically from the store window at the Spider's Web and strike bearish poses on the shelves at Another Catastrophe and the Quendale Mill. You might see them helping out at Shetland Islands Tourism or looking quaint and old-fashioned at the Shetland Museum. Maybe you'll spot them working in the gift shop on the Northlink ferries between Shetland and Aberdeen. Some have encountered them elsewhere in Great Britain—in Edinburgh, St. Andrews and Shropshire. They have names like Larry o' Lerwick, Thomas o' Tingwall, and Bobby o' Burrastow. Their soft, knitted bodies remind you of a favorite cardigan or pullover and their comical Fair Isle faces implore you to adopt them.

To find out more about these teddy bears masquerading as Fair Isle sweaters, we ventured out to Burra Isle to meet Wendy Inkster, creator of Burra Bears. Wendy emerges from her workshop to greet us, still wearing a work apron, followed close on heels by Sparky, her very energetic Jack Russell terrier. Wendy is as winsome as her bears, with tousled reddish hair and a dimpled smile. She invites us into her workshop where the bears are made. It's a cross between a toymaker's shop and a knitter's studio. Bins of Fair Isle sweaters line one wall, organized by color and pattern. The cutting table is against the window, which affords the bear-maker a magnificent ocean view. On shelves near the rear of the workshop sit the newest bears, patiently waiting to be shipped to their new homes. Each has a unique personality, depending on the colors used in its original sweater and the direction in which the pieces were cut. Most of these bears are so new, they haven't even gotten their name tags yet.

However, judging from the coos and squeals from those in our group, the adoption process for some could be expedited significantly.

They have names like Larry o' Lerwick, Thomas o' Tingwall, and Bobby o' Burrastow.

Once Wendy gets Sparky settled down, she explains how she got started in the Burra Bear business. Wanting to create a personal, rather than mass-produced, anniversary gift for her youngest sister, Wendy came up with the idea of using a shrunken Fair Isle sweater to make a pair of teddy bears. Naturally, these adorable bears stole the show at the anniversary party. Everyone wanted one. So, being energetic and enterprising, Wendy gathered old Fair Isle sweaters from family, friends and charity shops, and—once she had satisfied the demands of friends and family—was in business. She decided to call her creations Burra Bears. Soon, she was selling them at local shops and craft fairs.

Eventually, the bears—like the Fair Isle sweaters they're made of—found their way off the islands and began showing up in faraway places. One day, Wendy received a letter from a lady in South Africa who had received a Burra Bear from a friend. She wanted Wendy to

Please send a letter home to my Mummy so she knows where I've gone

Thankyou

know where the bear had gone to live. Now each bear comes with an envelope and reply card, which the new bear parent can send back to Wendy. Cards have come from as far away as Iceland, America, New Zealand, and Japan, and continue to come regularly from all over the world. New bear parents even send personalized cards and photos showing the bears in their new homes. Some want to know where other bears from the same town in Shetland have gone to live.

With all the international fame, Burra Bears is still very much a cottage industry. The business is growing, however, and Wendy already has two assistants. Even though she doesn't make every bear, Wendy shapes all the noses herself after they're made, to be sure each new bear has the unique Burra Bear look.

The bears have evolved from the original two, which were soft and floppy. Conventional toy stuffing, used in the two anniversary bears, didn't give Wendy the firmness she needed to shape the bears after assembly, so she began using knitting scraps for stuffing. This makes the bears truly 100% Fair Isle. She even uses the ribbing for ears and paws.

Asked why the bears all have men's names, Wendy replies, "to me they all look like little old Shetland men—this might have something to do with the shape of their tummies. I wanted their names to reflect this, so in the Shetland tradition, I give each bear a Christian name and a place name, like "Bertie o' Brough.""

Burra Bears have been so popular that Wendy recently launched a new bear—Yokel Bear—made from Fair Isle yoke sweaters, mainly plain with a Fair Isle pattern around the upper chest. Yokel Bears come complete with eyebrows, giving them many and varied expressions.

Needless to say, I was not immune to the charms of a certain bear. I left Burra Isle with Hamish o' Hamnavoe tucked safely away in my rucksack. He had a long trip ahead of him. He would have to cross the North Sea, ride the train from Aberdeen to Edinburgh and take two long flights to get to his new home in Northern California.

Gregory Courtney

"I'M OFTEN ASKED TO MAKE A BEAR FROM AN OLD SWEATER WHICH HAS SENTIMENTAL VALUE TO ITS OWNER—IT MAY HAVE BEEN A SWEATER THEY WORE WHEN THEY WERE LITTLE OR ONE THAT WAS HAND-KNITTED BY A RELATIVE—IT'S A GREAT WAY TO PRESERVE SOMETHING AND PASS IT ON DOWN THE GENERATIONS."

# kveldsro coat

*diane brown*

## MATERIALS

**YARN:** Jamieson's Soft Shetland - 1,050 (1,100, 1,150) grams. Shown in Midnight (1340).

**NEEDLES:** US 6 (4 mm) and US 7 (4.5 mm), *or correct needles to obtain gauge*.

**ACCESSORIES:** Seven 1" buttons (for buttonband) and two 1¼" matching buttons (for optional embellishment).

## MEASUREMENTS

**CHEST:** 46 (52, 56)".
**LENGTH:** 44 (46, 48)".
**SLEEVE LENGTH TO UNDERARM\*:** 17½ (18, 18½)".
**SLEEVE LENGTH TO SHOULDER\*:** 20½ (22½, 22¾)".
*\* Measured with cuff turned back.*

## GAUGE

On US 7 in st st: 20 sts and 28 rows = 4".

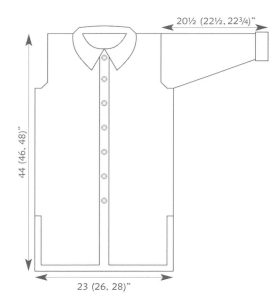

44 (46, 48)"

20½ (22½, 22¾)"

23 (26, 28)"

## MOSS RIB (MULTIPLE OF 4 + 1)
**Row 1 (RS):** K2; *p1, k3**; rep from * to ** to last 3 sts; end p1, k2.
**Row 2 (WS):** P1; *k3, p1**; rep from * to **.

Rep Rows 1-2.

## Moss Rib II (9 STS) (BUTTONBANDS & SIDE VENTS)
**Row 1 (RS):** K2; *p1, k3; end p1, k2.
**Row 2 (WS):** P1; ([k3, p1] twice).

Rep Rows 1-2.

## MAKE BUTTONHOLE
**Row 1 (RS):** K2, p1, BO 3 sts, p1, k2; knit to end.
**Row 2 (WS):** Purl to last 9 sts; p1, k2, CO 3 sts, k2, p1.

Rep Rows 1-2 for each buttonhole.

## BACK
With US 6, CO 121 (133, 141) sts. Beg with Row 2, work in **Moss Rib** for 2 (2, 2)", ending with RS facing for next row. Change to US 7.

**Next Row (RS):** Work first 9 (9, 9) sts in **Moss Rib II** as set; k103 (115, 123); work last 9 (9, 9) sts in **Moss Rib II** as set.
**Next Row (WS):** Work first 9 (9, 9) sts in **Moss Rib II** as set; p103 (115, 123); work last 9 (9, 9) sts in **Moss Rib II** as set.

Rep these 2 rows until piece measures 10 (10, 10)" from CO edge.

Continue in <u>st st only</u>, **AND AT SAME TIME**, dec 1 st at beg and end of every 24th (20th, 24th) row (on RS of work) 4 (5, 5) times as follows: k2, ssk, knit to last 4 sts, k2tog, k2. Continue without further shaping on rem 113 (123, 131) sts until piece measures 26 (27, 28)" from CO edge, ending with RS facing for next row.

## WAISTBAND

**Next Row (RS):** K37 (40, 42); place marker; work Row 1 of **Moss Rib** over next 39 (43, 47) sts; place marker; k37 (40, 42).

**Next Row (WS):** P37 (40, 42); work Row 2 of **Moss Rib** over next 39 (43, 47) sts (between markers); p37 (40, 42).

Continuing as set, rep these 2 rows 17 (17, 17) times, ending with RS facing for next row. Change to st st and work until piece measures 33½ (35, 36½)" from CO edge, ending with RS facing for next row.

## SHAPE ARMHOLES

BO 5 (5, 5) sts at beg of next 2 rows, then dec 1 st at beg and end of every RS row 6 (6, 7) times as follows: k2, ssk, knit to last 4 sts, k2tog, k2. Work without further shaping on rem 91 (101, 107) sts until armhole measures 10 (10½, 11)", ending with RS facing for next row.

**Next Row (RS):** K31 (33, 35), BO 29 (35, 37) sts, k31 (33, 35).

Turn, and working each side separately, BO 1 (1, 1) st at neck edge on next RS row. Place rem 30 (32, 34) sts on holders for shoulders.

## LEFT FRONT

With US 6, CO 61 (69, 77) sts. Beg with Row 2, work in **Moss Rib** for 2 (2, 2)", ending with RS facing for next row. Change to US 7.

**Next Row (RS):** Continue first 9 (9, 9) sts in **Moss Rib II** as set; k43 (51, 59); continue last 9 (9, 9) sts in **Moss Rib II** as set.

**Next Row (WS):** Continue first 9 (9, 9) sts in **Moss Rib II** as set; p43 (51, 59); continue last 9 (9, 9) sts in **Moss Rib II** as set.

Rep these 2 rows until piece measures 10 (10, 10)" from CO edge, ending with RS facing for next row.

**Next Row (RS):** K52 (60, 68); continue last 9 (9, 9) sts in **Moss Rib II** as set.

**Next Row (WS):** Continue first 9 (9, 9) sts in **Moss Rib II** as set; p52 (60, 68).

Rep these 2 rows, **AND AT SAME TIME**, dec 1 st at *beg* of every 24th (20th, 24th) row (on RS of work) 4 (5, 5) times as follows: k2, ssk, work to end of row. Continue without further shaping on rem 57 (64, 72) sts until piece measures 33½ (35, 36½)" from CO edge, ending with RS facing for next row.

## SHAPE ARMHOLE

BO 5 (5, 5) sts at beg of next row, then dec 1 st at *beg* of every RS row 6 (6, 7) times as follows: k2, ssk, work to end of row. Work without further shaping on rem 46 (53, 60) sts until armhole measures 7 (7½, 8)", ending with WS facing for next row.

## SHAPE NECK

**Next Row (WS):** Work 9 (9, 9) sts and place on holder, BO 0 (5, 5) sts, work to end of row.

Continuing as set, BO at neck edge 4 sts 1 (1, 1) time, 3 sts 0 (0, 1) time, 2 sts 0 (0, 1) time, then dec 1 st at neck edge on next 3 rows. Work without further shaping on rem 30 (32, 34) sts until armhole measures same as back. Place shoulder sts on holder.

## RIGHT FRONT

With US 6, CO 61 (69, 77) sts. Beg with Row 2, work in **Moss Rib** for 2 (2, 2)", ending with RS facing for next row. Change to US 7.

**Next Row (RS):** Continue first 9 (9, 9) sts in **Moss Rib II** as set; k43 (51, 59); continue last 9 (9, 9) sts in **Moss Rib II** as set.

**Next Row (WS):** Continue first 9 (9, 9) sts in **Moss Rib II** as set; p43 (51, 59); continue last 9 (9, 9) sts in **Moss Rib II** as set.

Rep these 2 rows until piece measures 10 (10, 10)" from CO edge, ending with RS facing for next row.

**Next Row (RS):** Continue first 9 (9, 9) sts in **Moss Rib II** as set; k52 (60, 68).

**Next Row (WS):** P52 (60, 68); continue last 9 (9, 9) sts in **Moss Rib II** as set.

Rep these 2 rows, **AND AT SAME TIME**, dec 1 st at *end* of every 24th (20th, 24th) row (on RS of work) 4 (5, 5) times as follows: work to last 4 sts, k2tog, k2.

ALSO AT SAME TIME, when front band measures 11 (11, 11)" from CO edge, **Make Buttonhole** every 5 (5, 5)", placing last buttonhole approximately 1 (1, 1)" below collar.

Continue without further shaping on rem 57 (64, 72) sts until piece measures 33½ (35, 36½)" from CO edge, ending with WS facing for next row.

## SHAPE ARMHOLE

BO 5 (5, 5) sts at beg of next row, then dec 1 st at *end* of every RS row 6 (6, 7) times as follows: work to last 4 sts;

k2tog, k2. Work without further shaping on rem 46 (53, 60) sts until armhole measures 7 (7½, 8)", ending with WS facing for next row.

### SHAPE NECK

**Next Row (RS):** Work 9 (9, 9) sts and place on holder, BO 0 (5, 5) sts, work to end of row.

Continuing as set, BO at neck edge 4 sts 1 (1, 1) time, 3 sts (0, 0, 1) time, 2 sts 0 (0, 1) time, then dec 1 st at neck edge on next 3 rows. Work without further shaping on rem 30 (32, 34) sts until armhole measures same as back. Place shoulder sts on holder.

### JOIN SHOULDERS

With RS's facing, join shoulders using 3-needle bind-off method.

### SLEEVES

With US 6, CO 65 (65, 65) sts. Work in **Moss Rib** for 4 (4, 4)", ending with RS facing for next row. Change to US 7 and work in st st, **AND AT SAME TIME**, inc 1 st at beg and end of every 4th row 12 (14, 16) times, then every 6th row 7 (7, 6) times (103 (107, 109) sts on needle). Work without further shaping until sleeve measures 17½ (18, 18½)" (with cuff turned back), ending with RS facing for next row.

### SHAPE SLEEVE CAP

BO 5 (5, 5) sts at beg of next 2 (2, 2) rows, 3 (3, 3) sts at beg of next 2 (2, 2) rows, 2 (2, 2) sts at beg of next 4 (6, 6) rows, dec 1 st at beg and end of every 7 (6, 6) rows, BO 2 (2, 2) sts at beg of next 6 (12, 12) rows, and 3 (3, 3) sts at beg of next 6 (2, 2) rows. BO rem 35 (37, 39) sts.

### COLLAR

With US 6, RS facing, beg at right front, continue 9 (9, 9) sts from holder in **Moss Rib II** as set; pick up 24 (24, 24) sts up right front neck, 31 (35, 39) sts along back neck edge, 24 (24, 24) sts down left front neck, continue 9 (9, 9) sts from holder in **Moss Rib II** as set (97 (101, 105) sts on needle).

**Next Row (WS):** Work Row 2 of **Moss Rib**.

Continue in **Moss Rib** as set until collar measures 7 (7, 7)". BO.

### FINISHING

Sew sleeves to armholes. Sew side seams, omitting side vents at bottom. Sew sleeve seams, reversing seam on last 2 (2, 2)" of cuff. Turn cuff back. Sew smaller buttons opposite buttonholes. Sew larger buttons just above slits on sides, if desired. Weave in ends. Block to finished measurements.

# barclay vest

*gregory courtney*

## MATERIALS

**YARN:** Jamieson's Shetland Double Knitting - 100 (100, 150, 150) grams each of Color A, Color B and Color C. Shown in Color A, Admiral Navy (727); Color B, Coffee (880); and Color C, Tundra (190).
**NEEDLES:** 20" circular US 4 (3.5 mm) and 32" circular US 6 (4 mm), *or correct needles to obtain gauge.*
**ACCESSORIES:** Stitch holders.

## MEASUREMENTS

**CHEST:** 40 (44, 48, 52)".
**LENGTH TO ARMHOLE:** 14½ (15, 15½, 16)".
**ARMHOLE DEPTH:** 9½ (10, 10½, 11)".
**LENGTH:** 24 (25, 26, 27)".

## GAUGE

On US 6 in **3-Color Box Stitch**: 20 sts and 32 rows = 4".

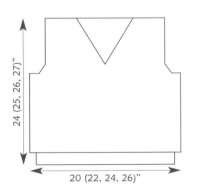

24 (25, 26, 27)"

20 (22, 24, 26)"

## 3-COLOR BOX STITCH (MULTIPLE OF 4 + 2)

**Row 1 (RS):** With Color A, *k2, p2**; rep from * to **; end k2.
**Row 2 (WS):** With Color B, *k2, p2**; rep from * to **; end k2.
**Row 3 (RS):** With Color C, *k2, p2**; rep from * to **; end k2.
**Row 4 (WS):** With Color A, *k2, p2**; rep from * to **; end k2.
**Row 5 (RS):** With Color B, *k2, p2**; rep from * to **; end k2.
**Row 6 (WS):** With Color C, *k2, p2**; rep from * to **; end k2.

Rep Rows 1-6.

## BACK

With US 4 and Color A, CO 102 (110, 122, 130) sts.

**Row 1 (WS):** With Color A, *p2, k2**; rep from * to **; end p2.
**Row 2 (RS):** With Color B, *k2, p2**; rep from * to **; end k2.
**Row 3 (WS):** With Color B, *p2, k2**; rep from * to **; end p2.
**Row 4 (RS):** With Color C, *k2, p2**; rep from * to **; end k2.
**Row 5 (WS):** With Color C, *p2, k2**; rep from * to **; end p2.
**Row 6 (RS):** With Color A, *k2, p2**; rep from * to **; end k2.
**Row 7 (WS):** With Color A, *p2, k2**; rep from * to **; end p2.

Rep Rows 2-7 once more, then work Rows 2-5 once more.

Change to US 6 and work **3-Color Box Stitch** until work measures 14½ (15, 15½, 16)" from CO edge, ending with RS facing for next row.

### SHAPE ARMHOLES

BO 8 (8, 8, 8) sts at beg of next 2 rows, then dec 1 (1, 1, 1) st at beg and end of every RS row 8 (8, 8, 8) times.

Work without further shaping on rem 70 (78, 90, 98) sts until armhole measures 9½ (10, 10½, 11)", ending with RS facing for next row.

**Next Row (RS):** BO 18 (22, 26, 30) sts; work 34 (34, 38, 38) sts and place on holder for back neck; BO 18 (22, 26, 30) sts.

### FRONT
Work same as for back until armhole shaping is complete, ending with RS facing for next row.

### SHAPE NECK
**Next Row (RS):** Work 34 (38, 44, 48) sts and place on holder; work next 2 sts and place on safety pin; work 34 (38, 44, 48) sts.

Turn, and working each side separately, dec 1 st at neck edge on next RS row, then every 4th row 15 (15, 17, 17) more times (16 (16, 18, 18) times total). Work without further shaping on rem 18 (22, 26, 30) sts until piece is same length as back. BO.

### JOIN SHOULDERS
Sew shoulders tog on WS using back stitch.

### ARMBANDS
With US 4 and Color A, RS facing, beg at underarm, pick up 57 (61, 65, 69) sts along armhole to shoulder seam and 57 (61, 65, 69) sts from shoulder seam along armhole to underarm (114 (122 130, 138) sts on needle).

**Row 1 (WS):** With Color A, *p2, k2**; rep from * to **; end p2.
**Row 2 (RS):** With Color B, *k2, p2**; rep from * to **; end k2.

**Row 3 (WS):** With Color B, *p2, k2**; rep from * to **; end p2.
**Row 4 (RS):** With Color C, *k2, p2**; rep from * to **; end k2.
**Row 5 (WS):** With Color C, *p2, k2**; rep from * to **; end p2.
**Row 6 (RS):** With Color A, *k2, p2**; rep from * to **; end k2.
**Row 7 (WS):** With Color A, *p2, k2**; rep from * to **; end p2.

With Color A, BO in pattern.

### NECKBAND
With 20" circular US 4 and Color A, RS facing, beg at right shoulder, pick up 2 (2, 2, 2) sts at right shoulder seam, k34 (34, 38, 38) sts from back neck holder, pick up 2 (2, 2, 2) sts at left shoulder seam, pick up 44 (44, 48, 48) sts down left neck edge, place marker, knit 2 (2, 2, 2) sts from holder, place marker, pick up 44 (44, 48, 48) sts up right neck edge (128 (128, 140, 140) sts on needle). Join, and with Color A, work in the rnd as follows:

**Rnd 1:** *P2, k2**; rep from * to ** to 2 sts before marker; p2tog, slip marker, k2, slip marker, p2tog; *k2, p2**; rep from * to ** to last 2 sts; end k2.

Continuing rib as set and working left- and right-slanting decs before 1st marker and after 2nd marker on every rnd, work 2 rows in Color B, 2 rows in Color C, and 2 rows in Color A. With Color A, BO in pattern.

### FINISHING
Sew side seams and armbands at underarms. Weave in ends. Block to finished measurements.

# r u a n a

*cc conway*

## MATERIALS

**YARN:** Jamieson's Shetland Double Knitting - 325 grams of
MC, Black (999); 100 grams each of Color A, Pistachio (791);
Color B, Old Gold (429); and Color C, Olive (825).
**NEEDLES:** US 5 (3.75 mm), *or correct needle to obtain gauge.*

## MEASUREMENTS
**WIDTH:** 40".
**LENGTH:** 27½".

## GAUGE
On US 5 in garter st: 24 sts = 4".

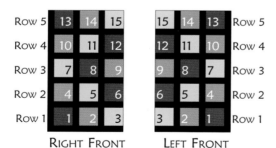

**BACK**

| Row 1 | | | | | | |
|---|---|---|---|---|---|---|
| 7 | 6 | 5 | 4 | 3 | 2 | 1 |
| 14 | 13 | 12 | 11 | 10 | 9 | 8 | Row 2
| 21 | 20 | 19 | 18 | 17 | 16 | 15 | Row 3
| 28 | 27 | 26 | 25 | 24 | 23 | 22 | Row 4
| 35 | 34 | 33 | 32 | 31 | 30 | 29 | Row 5

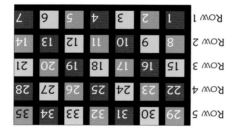

| Row 5 | 13 | 14 | 15 |
| Row 4 | 10 | 11 | 12 |
| Row 3 | 7 | 8 | 9 |
| Row 2 | 4 | 5 | 6 |
| Row 1 | 1 | 2 | 3 |

**RIGHT FRONT**

| 15 | 14 | 13 | Row 5 |
| 12 | 11 | 10 | Row 4 |
| 9 | 8 | 7 | Row 3 |
| 6 | 5 | 4 | Row 2 |
| 3 | 2 | 1 | Row 1 |

**LEFT FRONT**

## COLOR KEY

BEG w/BLACK (999); CHANGE TO PISTACHIO (791)

BEG w/BLACK (999); CHANGE TO OLD GOLD (429)

BEG w/BLACK (999); CHANGE TO OLIVE (825)

## NOTE
When pattern calls for sts to be "picked up," be sure RS of
square is facing.

## BASIC SQUARE PATTERN
*Worked on 57 sts on US 5. Beg Row 1 below with MC
and work 9 garter ridges, then change to color indicated
for remainder of square.*

**Row 1 (WS):** Knit to last st; p1.
**Row 2 (RS):** Sl1 kwise, knit to center 3 sts, sl1, k2tog,
psso, knit to last st, p1 (mark this side so you know it's the
RS).
**Row 3 (and all rem WS rows):** Sl1 kwise, knit to last st,
p1.

Rep Rows 2 and 3, **AND AT SAME TIME**, when there are
9 garter ridges, change to color indicated on **Chart.** When
5 sts rem, work as follows:

**Next Row (RS):** Sl1 kwise, sl1, k2tog, psso, p1.
**Next Row (WS):** Sl1 kwise, k1, p1.
**Next Row (RS):** Sl1 kwise, k2tog, psso.

One st rems. *Depending on orientation of square and
next square to be worked, this st will either be left open
to be worked with next square, or yarn will be pulled
through st if last square in row.*

## BACK
**Note:** Refer to **Back Chart** for colors and sequences.

## Row 1
**Square 1:** With US 5 and MC, work **Basic Square Pattern**,
ending with 1 st rem on needle. Leave last rem st open
and remove from needle. Tilt square so diagonal line in
middle of square slants from bottom left to top right.

**Squares 2-7:** With MC, CO 28 sts, pick up 28 sts along
right edge of previous square, place st from previous
square onto needle (57 sts on needle). Work **Basic Square
Pattern.** Leave last rem st open and remove from needle.
*If last square in row, pull yarn through last rem st.*

### Row 2
**Square 8:** With MC, pick up 28 sts along top of left-most square in previous row, CO 29 sts (57 sts on needle). Work **Basic Square Pattern**. Leave last rem st open and rem from needle.

**Squares 9-14:** With MC, pick up 28 sts along top of square below, pick up 28 sts along right edge of previous square. Place last rem st from previous square onto needle (57 sts on needle). Work **Basic Square Pattern**. Leave last rem st open and rem from needle. *If last square in row, pull yarn through last rem st.*

### Rows 3-5 (Squares 15-35)
Work in same manner as in Row 2.

### RIGHT FRONT
**Note:** Refer to **Right Front Chart** for colors and sequences.

### Row 1
Work in same manner as in Row 1 of back.

### Row 2
Work in same manner as in Row 2 of back.

### Rows 3-5
Work in same manner as in Rows 3-5 of back.

### LEFT FRONT
**Note:** Refer to **Left Front Chart** for colors and sequences.

### Row 1
**Square 1:** With US 5 and MC, work **Basic Square Pattern**, ending with 1 st on needle. Leave last rem st on needle. Tilt square so diagonal line in middle of square slants from bottom right to top left.

**Squares 2-3:** With last st of previous square still on needle, with MC, pick up 28 sts along left side of previous square, CO 28 (57 sts on needle). Work **Basic Square Pattern**. Leave last rem st on needle. *If last square in row, pull yarn through last rem st.*

### Row 2
**Square 4:** With MC, CO 28 sts, pick up 29 sts along top of right-most square in previous square (57 sts on needle). Work **Basic Square Pattern**. Leave last rem st on needle.

**Squares 5-6:** With last rem st from previous square still on needle, pick up 28 sts along left side of previous square, pick up 28 sts along top of square below (57 sts on needle). Work **Basic Square Pattern**. Leave last rem st on needle. *If last square in row, pull yarn through last rem st.*

### Rows 3-5 (Squares 7-15)
Work in same manner as in Row 2.

### FINISHING
With US 5 and MC, RS facing, pick up 140 sts along right edge of back. Work 9 garter ridges. BO.

### JOIN SHOULDERS
With US 5 and MC, RS facing, pick up 84 sts along top of left front. Work 4 garter ridges. Leave sts on needle. With another US 5, RS facing, pick up 84 sts along 3 left-most squares of back. Work 4 garter ridges. With WS's facing, join using 3-needle bind-off method. Rep for right shoulder on 3 right-most squares.

### FRONT BORDER
With US 5 and MC, RS facing, pick up 150 sts from bottom of right front to shoulder seam, 49 sts along back neck edge, and 150 sts from shoulder seam to bottom of left front (349 sts on needle). Work 9 garter ridges. BO.

Work single crochet around entire edge of piece. Weave in ends. Block to finished measurements.

# nicola pullover

*beatrice smith*

## MATERIALS

**YARN:** Jamieson's Soft Shetland - 500 (500, 550, 600) grams. Shown in Amethyst (1310).
**NEEDLES:** 16" circular US 5 (3.75 mm) and 32" circular US 6 (4 mm), *or correct needles to obtain gauge.*
**ACCESSORIES:** Stitch holders.

## MEASUREMENTS

**CHEST:** 37 (40, 44, 47)".
**LENGTH:** 22 (22½, 23, 23½)".
**SLEEVE LENGTH TO UNDERARM:** 16½ (16½, 17½, 17½)".
**SLEEVE LENGTH TO SHOULDER:** 18 (18, 19, 19)".

## GAUGE

On US 6 in **Pattern Stitch**: 19 sts and 26 rows = 4".

**PATTERN STITCH (MULTIPLE OF 8 STS)**
Rows 1, 3 & 5 (RS): *P3, k5**; rep from * to **.
Rows 2, 4 & 6 (WS): *P5, k3**; rep from * to **.
Rows 7, 9 & 11 (RS): *K5, p3**; rep from * to **.
Rows 8, 10 & 12 (WS): *K3, p5**; rep from * to **.

Rep Rows 1-12.

**BACK**
With US 6, CO 88 (96, 104, 112) sts.

Next Row (WS): Purl.
Next Row (RS): Knit.
Next Row (WS): Purl.

Work in **Pattern Stitch** until piece measures 13 (13, 13, 13)" from CO edge, ending with RS facing for next row.

**SHAPE ARMHOLES**
BO 4 (4, 4, 4) sts at beg of next 2 rows, then dec 1 st at beg and end of every RS row 4 (4, 4, 4) times. Work without further shaping on rem 72 (80, 88, 96) sts until piece measures 21 (21½, 22, 22½)" from CO edge, ending with RS facing for next row.

**SHAPE NECK**
Next Row (RS): Work 24 (27, 30, 34) sts and place on holder; work 24 (26, 28, 28) sts and place on another holder for back neck; work 24 (27, 30, 34) sts.

Turn, and working each side separately, BO at neck edge 3 (3, 3, 3) sts 1 (1, 1, 1) time, 2 (2, 2, 2) sts 1 (1, 1, 1) time, then dec 1 (1, 1, 1) st 1 (1, 1, 1) time. Work without further shaping on rem 18 (21, 24, 28) sts until piece measures 22 (22½, 23, 23½)" from CO edge. Place sts on holders for shoulders.

**FRONT**
Work same as for back until piece measures 19 (19½, 20, 20½)" from CO edge, ending with RS facing for next row.

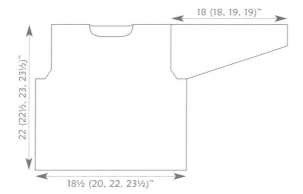

# nicola pullover

### Shape Neck
**Next Row (RS):** Work 28 (31, 34, 38) sts and place on holder; work 16 (18, 20, 20) sts and place on another holder for front neck; work 28 (31, 34, 38) sts.

Turn, and working each side separately, BO at neck edge 3 (3, 3, 3) sts 1 (1, 1, 1) time, 2 (2, 2, 2) sts 2 (2, 2, 2) times, then dec 1 (1, 1, 1) st 3 (3, 3, 3) times. Work without further shaping on rem 18 (21, 24, 28) sts until piece measures 22 (22½, 23, 23½)" from CO edge. Place shoulder sts on holders.

### Join Shoulders
With RS's facing, join shoulders using 3-needle bind-off method.

### Sleeves
With US 6, CO 51 (51, 51, 51) sts.

**Next Row (WS):** Purl.
**Next Row (RS):** Knit.
**Next Row (WS):** Purl.

**Row 1 (RS):** *P3, k5**; rep from * to ** to last 3 sts; p3.
**Row 2 (WS):** *K3, p5**; rep from * to ** to last 3 sts; k3.

Continuing as set, work in **Pattern Stitch, AND AT SAME TIME,** inc 1 st at beg and end of next row, then every 4th row 0 (4, 11, 15) times, then every 6th row 15 (14, 10, 8) times, working inc'd sts into **Pattern Stitch** (83 (89, 95, 99) sts on needle). Work without further shaping until piece measures approx. 16½ (16½, 17½, 17½)" from CO edge, ending after working Row 2 of **Pattern Stitch.**

### Shape Sleeve Cap
BO 4 (4, 4, 4) sts at beg of next 2 rows, then dec 1 st at beg and end of every RS row 4 (4, 4, 4) times (67 (73, 79, 83) sts on needle). After last dec row, work 1 WS row, then BO.

### Neckband
With 16" circular US 5, RS facing, beg at right shoulder seam, pick up 8 (8, 8, 8) sts to back neck holder; k24 (26, 28, 28) sts from back neck holder; pick up 8 (8, 8, 8) sts to left shoulder seam; pick up 14 (14, 14, 14) sts down left neck edge; k16 (18, 20, 20) sts from front neck holder; pick up 14 (14, 14, 14) sts up right neck edge (84 (88, 92, 92) sts on needle). Join, and work in k2, p2 rib for 3 rnds, then work in st st for 5 rnds. BO.

### Finishing
Sew sleeves to body. Sew side and sleeve seams. Weave in ends. Block *gently* to finished measurements (***don't overblock! If you do, you'll lose the soft undulating ribs formed by the pattern stitch***).

# falling leaves scarf

*sandi rosner*

---

## MATERIALS
YARN: Jamieson's Shetland 2-Ply Spindrift - 75 grams.
Shown in Ginger (462).
NEEDLES: Circular 24" US 4 (3.5 mm),
*or correct needle to obtain gauge.*

## MEASUREMENTS
WIDTH: Approx. 10" (after blocking).
LENGTH: Approx. 48" (after blocking).

## GAUGE
On US 4 in **Chart B**: 30 sts = 4¼" and 40 rows = 5¾".

---

## ABOUT CHARTS
Read odd-numbered (RS) rows from right to left and even-numbered (WS) rows from left to right.

## DESIGNER NOTES
Work **Bottom Border** (**Chart A**) first. Pick up along edge of **Bottom Border** and work side borders (**Chart A** and **Chart C**) along with center leaf pattern (**Chart B**). Join **Top Border** (**Chart D**) to **Scarf Body** as you knit it.

## SCARF
### BOTTOM BORDER
With US 4, using provisional cast-on method, CO 8 sts.

**Next Row (WS):** Purl.

Work Rows 1-12 of **Chart A** 6 times, then work Rows 1-2 once more (7 sts on needle).

## SCARF BODY
With WS facing, pick up and purl 48 sts along the straight side of **Bottom Border**, then recover 7 sts from provisional CO (62 sts on needle).

Work Row 3 of **Chart C**; place marker; ([k2tog, yo] 24 times); place marker; work Row 3 of **Chart A**.
Work Row 4 of **Chart A**; p48; work Row 4 of **Chart C**.

Continuing borders as established, with **Chart C** for right side border and **Chart A** for left side border, work **Chart B** over center 48 sts. Work **Chart B** 30 times, then work Rows 1-8 of **Chart B** again (Row 12 of borders completed).

Work Row 1 of **Chart C**; ([k2tog, yo] 24 times); work Row 1 of **Chart A**.

Work Row 2 of **Chart A**; remove marker; ([p2, p2tog] 12 times); remove marker; work Row 2 of **Chart C** (50 sts on needle).

## TOP BORDER
Work Rows 3-12 of **Chart D**; ([work Rows 1-12 of **Chart D**] 5 times), joining border to center section of scarf by knitting last stitch of border tog with one stitch of body at end of every odd-numbered row, and slipping the first stitch of every even-numbered row.

Work Row 1 of **Chart D** once more.

Graft rem 7 sts of **Top Border** to 7 stitches at top of left side border.

## FINISHING
Weave in ends. Block to finished measurements, pinning out points of border.

## Chart A - Bottom Border & Left Border

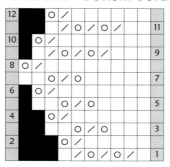

## Chart C - Right Border

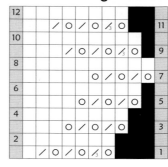

## Chart B - Center Leaf Pattern

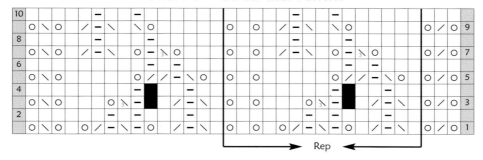

Rep

## Chart D - Top Border

## Key

| | |
|---|---|
| ☐ | k on right side rows; p on wrong side rows. |
| — | p on right side rows; k on wrong side rows. |
| ╱ | k2tog. |
| ╲ | ssk. |
| ○ | yo. |
| ⟍ | sl1, k2tog, psso. |
| ⟋ | k3tog. |
| ⌢ | sl1 wyif. |
| ■ | no stitch. |

# kaleidoscope 2 jacket

*carol lapin*

## MATERIALS

**YARN:** Jamieson's Shetland Double Knitting - 150 grams each of Rust (578) and Sunrise (187); 100 grams each of Burnt Umber (1190); Loganberry (1290); Maroon (595); Old Gold (429); Peacock (258); and Rosemary (821); 50 grams of Black (999).
**NEEDLES:** US 6 (4 mm), *or correct needle to obtain gauge.* Pair of short double-pointed US 8 (5 mm).

## MEASUREMENTS
**CHEST:** 60".
**LENGTH:** 27".

## GAUGE
On US 6 in garter st: 21 sts and 42 rows = 4".

## DESIGNER NOTES
Work jacket body in 12 separate panels and sleeves in 2 separate panels each. Pick up sts along edges of adjacent panels and join tog using **3-Needle Bind-off Method**. "Garter ridge" means 2 rows.

## 3-NEEDLE BIND-OFF METHOD
With WS's facing, hold needles parallel. *With 3rd needle, knit tog 1st st of needle 1 with 1st st of needle 2; knit tog 2nd st of needle 1 with 2nd st of needle 2; pass 1st st over 2nd st (BO)**; rep from * to ** until 1 st rems. Pull yarn through last rem st.

## APPLIED CORDED EDGING
With short double-pointed US 8 and Sunrise, CO 3 sts. With same needle, WS facing, *pick up 1 st; slide all 4 sts to opposite end of needle; k2, k2togtbl**; rep from * to **.

## COLOR SEQUENCE FOR PANELS 1 & 2 (BOTTOM TO TOP)

| | |
|---|---|
| 6 garter ridges Loganberry | 4 garter ridges Old Gold |
| 8 garter ridges Old Gold | 7 garter ridges Sunrise |
| 1 garter ridge Rust | 3 garter ridges Loganberry |
| 4 garter ridges Maroon | 4 garter ridges Rosemary |
| 1 garter ridge Rust | 6 garter ridges Rust |
| 3 garter ridges Burnt Umber | 4 garter ridges Burnt Umber |
| 7 garter ridges Rosemary | 1 garter ridge Maroon |
| 5 garter ridges Loganberry | 5 garter ridges Peacock |
| 3 garter ridges Sunrise | 1 garter ridge Maroon |
| 2 garter ridges Peacock | 3 garter ridges Sunrise |
| 6 garter ridges Old Gold | 6 garter ridges Old Gold |
| 2 garter ridges Burnt Umber | 6 garter ridges Loganberry |
| 6 garter ridges Rust | 4 garter ridges Maroon |
| 3 garter ridges Maroon | 3 garter ridges Rosemary |
| 1 garter ridge Loganberry | End with Rosemary |
| 5 garter ridges Peacock | |

## COLOR SEQUENCE FOR PANELS 3 & 4 (BOTTOM TO TOP)

| | |
|---|---|
| 6 garter ridges Loganberry | 5 garter ridges Peacock |
| 8 garter ridges Old Gold | 4 garter ridges Old Gold |
| 1 garter ridge Rust | 7 garter ridges Sunrise |
| 4 garter ridges Maroon | 3 garter ridges Loganberry |
| 1 garter ridge Rust | 4 garter ridges Rosemary |
| 3 garter ridges Burnt Umber | 6 garter ridges Rust |
| 7 garter ridges Rosemary | 4 garter ridges Burnt Umber |
| 5 garter ridges Loganberry | 1 garter ridge Maroon |
| 3 garter ridges Sunrise | 5 garter ridges Peacock |
| 2 garter ridges Peacock | 1 garter ridge Maroon |
| 6 garter ridges Old Gold | 3 garter ridges Sunrise |
| 2 garter ridges Burnt Umber | 6 garter ridges Old Gold |
| 6 garter ridges Rust | 4 garter ridges Loganberry |
| 3 garter ridges Maroon | End with Loganberry |
| 1 garter ridge Loganberry | |

## COLOR SEQUENCE FOR SLEEVE PANELS 1 & 2 (SHOULDER TO CUFF)

| | |
|---|---|
| 7 garter ridges Sunrise | 2 garter ridges Loganberry |
| 3 garter ridges Loganberry | 5 garter ridges Maroon |
| 4 garter ridges Rosemary | 3 garter ridges Old Gold |
| 6 garter ridges Rust | 4 garter ridges Peacock |
| 4 garter ridges Burnt Umber | 3 garter ridges Sunrise |
| 1 garter ridge Maroon | 2 garter ridges Loganberry |
| 5 garter ridges Peacock | 6 garter ridges Rust |
| 1 garter ridge Maroon | 4 garter ridges Rosemary |
| 3 garter ridges Sunrise | 3 garter ridges Maroon |
| 4 garter ridges Old Gold | 4 garter ridges Old Gold |
| 6 garter ridges Rust | 2 garter ridges Loganberry |
| 2 garter ridges Burnt Umber | End with Loganberry |
| 4 garter ridges Rosemary | |

# kaleidoscope 2 jacket

## PANEL 1 (MAKE 5)

With US 6 and Loganberry, CO 2 sts. Following **Color Sequence for Panels 1 and 2** throughout, work as follows:

**Row 1 (WS):** Knit.
**Row 2 (RS):** Knit into front and back of both sts (4 sts on needle).
**Row 3 (WS):** Sl1 kwise, knit to last st, p1.
**Row 4 (RS):** Sl1 kwise, m1, knit to last 2 sts, knit into front and back of next st, p1.

Rep Rows 3-4 until there are 34 sts on needle, ending with RS facing for next row (holding piece, RS facing, so Loganberry triangle is in bottom **left** corner, bottom edge should measure approx. 4½").

**Next Row (RS):** Sl1 kwise, k2tog, knit to last st, m1, p1.
**Next Row (WS):** Sl1 kwise, knit to last st, p1.

Rep the above 2 rows until piece measures approx. 27" along longest side and 3 ridges of last occurrence of Old Gold have been worked, ending with RS facing for next row.

### SQUARE OFF AND CLOSE PANEL

**Next Row (RS):** Sl1 kwise, k2tog, knit to last 3 sts, k2tog, p1.
**Next Row (WS):** Sl1 kwise, knit to last st, p1.

Rep the above 2 rows until 3 sts rem, ending with RS facing for next row.

**Next Row (RS):** K2tog, p1.
**Next Row (WS):** Sl1 kwise, p1.
**Next Row (RS):** K2tog. Pull yarn through last rem st.

## PANEL 2 (MAKE 5)

Work same as for **Panel 1** until there are 34 sts on needle, ending with RS facing for next row (holding piece, RS facing, so Loganberry triangle is in bottom **right** corner, bottom edge should measure approx. 4½").

**Next Row (RS):** Sl1 kwise, m1, knit to last 3 sts, k2tog, p1.
**Next Row (WS):** Sl1 kwise, knit to last st, p1.

Rep the above 2 rows until piece measures approx. 27" along longest side and 3 ridges of last occurrence of Old Gold have been worked, ending with RS facing for next row.

Work **Square Off and Close Panel** instructions same as for **Panel 1**.

## PANEL 3 (MAKE 1)

Work same as for **Panel 1** (working **Color Sequence for Panels 3 & 4**) until there are 34 sts on needle, ending with RS facing for next row (holding piece, RS facing, so Loganberry triangle is in bottom **left** corner, bottom edge should measure approx. 4½").

**Next Row (RS):** Sl1 kwise, k2tog, knit to last st, m1, p1.
**Next Row (WS):** Sl1 kwise, knit to last st, p1.

Rep the above 2 rows until longest side of piece measures 12", ending with RS facing for next row.

**Row 1 (RS):** Sl1 kwise, k3tog, knit to last st, m1, p1.
**Rows 2, 4, 6 & 8 (WS):** Sl1 kwise, knit to last st, p1.
**Rows 3, 5 & 7 (RS):** Sl1 kwise, k2tog, knit to last st, m1, p1.

Rep Rows 1-8 above until 19 sts rem, ending with RS facing for next row.

Work **Square Off and Close Panel** instructions same as for **Panel 1**.

## PANEL 4 (MAKE 1)

Work same as for **Panel 1** (working **Color Sequence for Panels 3 & 4**) until there are 34 sts on needle, ending with RS facing for next row (holding piece, RS facing, so Loganberry triangle is in bottom **right** corner, bottom edge should measure approx. 4½").

**Next Row (RS):** Sl1 kwise, m1, knit to last 3 sts, k2tog, p1.
**Next Row (WS):** Sl1 kwise, knit to last st, p1.

Rep the above 2 rows until longest side of piece measures 12", ending with RS facing for next row.

**Row 1 (RS):** Sl1 kwise, m1, knit to last 4 sts, k3tog, p1.
**Rows 2, 4, 6 & 8 (WS):** Sl1 kwise, knit to last st, p1.
**Rows 3, 5 & 7 (RS):** Sl1 kwise, m1, knit to last 3 sts, k2tog, p1.

Rep the above 8 rows until 19 sts rem, ending with RS facing for next row.

Work **Square Off and Close Panel** instructions same as for **Panel 1**.

## SLEEVE PANEL 1 (MAKE 2)

With US 6 and Sunrise, CO 2 sts. Following **Color Sequence for Sleeves** throughout, work as follows:

**Row 1 (WS):** Knit.

# kaleidoscope 2 jacket

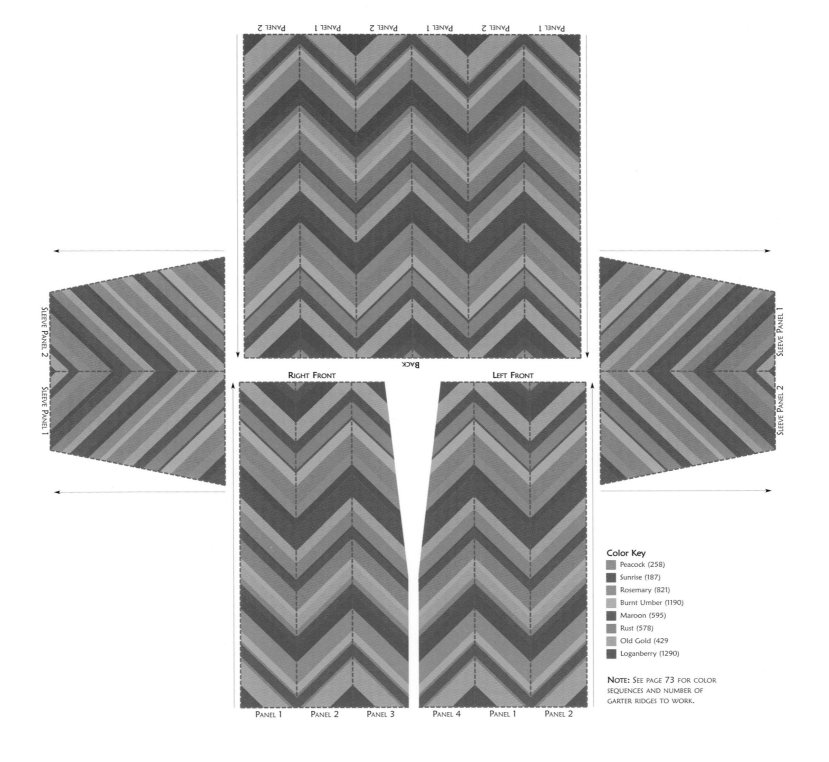

Panel 2   Panel 1   Panel 2   Panel 1   Panel 2   Panel 1

Sleeve Panel 2

Sleeve Panel 1

Sleeve Panel 1

Sleeve Panel 2

Back

Right Front          Left Front

Panel 1   Panel 2   Panel 3   Panel 4   Panel 1   Panel 2

**Color Key**

- Peacock (258)
- Sunrise (187)
- Rosemary (821)
- Burnt Umber (1190)
- Maroon (595)
- Rust (578)
- Old Gold (429)
- Loganberry (1290)

**Note:** See page 73 for color sequences and number of garter ridges to work.

**Row 2 (RS):** Knit into front and back of both sts (4 sts on needle).
**Row 3 (WS):** Sl1 kwise, knit to last st, p1.
**Row 4 (RS):** Sl1 kwise, m1, knit to last 2 sts, knit into front and back of next st, p1.

Rep Rows 3-4, **AND AT SAME TIME,** omit inc at **end** of Row 4 every 3rd garter ridge (6th row) (this is the same as a dec on a conventional sleeve worked from the top down) until there are 64 sts.

**Row 1 (RS):** Sl1 kwise, k2tog, knit to last st, m1, p1.
**Row 2 (WS):** Sl1 kwise, knit to last st, p1.
**Row 3 (RS):** Sl1 kwise, k2tog, knit to last st, p1.
**Row 4 (WS):** Sl1 kwise, knit to last st, p1.

Rep Rows 1-4 above until the longest side of piece measures 15", ending with RS facing for next row.

Work **Square Off and Close Panel** instructions same as for **Panel 1.**

## SLEEVE PANEL 2 (MAKE 2)
Work same as for **Sleeve Panel 1,** omitting inc at **beg** of Row 4 every 3rd garter ridge (6th row) (this is the same as a dec on a conventional sleeve worked from the top down) until there are 64 sts.

**Row 1 (RS):** Sl1 kwise, m1, knit to last 3 sts, k2tog, p1.
**Row 2 (WS):** Sl1 kwise, knit to last st, p1.
**Row 3 (RS):** Sl1 kwise, knit to last 3 sts, k2tog, p1.
**Row 4 (WS):** Sl1 kwise, knit to last st, p1.

Rep Rows 1-4 above until the longest side of piece measures 15", ending with RS facing for next row.

Work **Square Off and Close Panel** instructions same as for **Panel 1.**

## JOIN BACK PANELS
**NOTE:** See schematic for placement of panels.

With US 6 and Sunrise, RS facing, pick up 106 sts along edge of panel. With another US 6, pick up 106 sts along edge of adjacent panel. With WS's facing, join using **3-Needle Bind-off Method.** Rep until all panels of back are joined.

## JOIN LEFT FRONT & RIGHT FRONT PANELS
Join same as for back panels.

## JOIN SHOULDERS
With US 6 and Sunrise, RS facing, pick up 46 sts along top of back right shoulder. With another US 6, pick up 46 sts along top or front right shoulder. With WS's facing, join using **3-Needle Bind-off Method.** Rep for left shoulder.

## JOIN SLEEVES HALVES
With US 6 and Sunrise, RS facing, pick up 54 sts along straight edge of **Sleeve Panel 1.** With another US 6, pick up 54 sts along straight edge of **Sleeve Panel 2.** With WS's facing, join using **3-Needle Bind-off Method.** Rep for other sleeve.

## JOIN SLEEVES TO BODY
With US 6 and Sunrise, RS facing, pick up 38 sts along top of sleeve to center seam, pick up 1 st in center seam, pick up 38 sts along top of sleeve (77 sts on needle). With another US 6, pick up 38 sts up body to shoulder seam, pick up 1 st in shoulder seam, pick up 38 sts down body (77 sts on needle). With WS's facing, join using **3-Needle Bind-off Method.**

## JOIN SIDE SEAMS
With US 6 and Sunrise, RS facing, pick up 68 sts along left seam edge of back. With another US 6, pick up 68 sts along seam edge of left front. With WS's facing, join using **3-Needle Bind-off Method.** Rep to join back to right front.

## JOIN SLEEVE SEAMS
With US 6 and Sunrise, RS facing, pick up 60 sts along seam edge of sleeve. With another US 6, pick up 60 sts along other seam edge. With WS's facing, join using **3-Needle Bind-off Method.** Rep for other sleeve.

## FRONT BAND
With US 6 and Sunrise, CO 30 sts. Working in st st throughout, *work 2 rows Sunrise, work 2 rows Black**; rep from * to ** until band fits comfortably along front edges and around neck (approx. 60"). Fold in half and sew to jacket.

## BOTTOM AND SLEEVE EDGING
Work **Applied Corded Edging** around bottom of jacket. Rep for sleeve cuffs.

Weave in ends. Block to finished measurements.

# cosmos jacket

*nadine shapiro*

## MATERIALS

**YARN:** Jamieson's Shetland Double Knitting - 250 grams of Color A, Port Wine (293); 200 grams of Color B, Maroon (595); 50 grams each of Color C, Rust (578) and Color D, Plum (585)

**NEEDLES:** 32" circular US 5 (3.75 mm) and 32" circular US 6 (4 mm) *or correct needles to obtain gauge.* G crochet hook.

**ACCESSORIES:** Stitch holders.

## MEASUREMENTS

CHEST: 46".
LENGTH: 22".
SLEEVE LENGTH: 17".

## GAUGE

On US 6 in st st: 20 sts and 28 rows = 4".

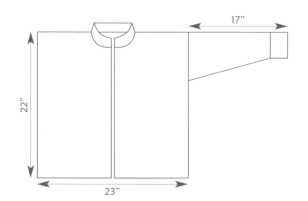

## DESIGNER NOTES

Begin back and fronts with provisional cast-on. Work the bottom border downwards.

## ABOUT CHARTS

Read odd-numbered (RS) rows from right to left and even-numbered (WS) rows from left to right. Work **Back Chart**, **Right Front Chart** and **Left Front Chart** using intarsia method. Work **Sleeve Cuff Chart**, **Bottom Border Chart** and **Collar Chart** using "Fair Isle" or stranded method.

## BACK

With G crochet hook and waste yarn, loosely chain approx. 120 sts. With US 6 and Color A, pick up 115 sts along underside of chain, leaving extra chains to be removed later. Work the 138 rows of **Back Chart**. BO.

## LEFT FRONT

With G crochet hook and waste yarn, loosely chain approximately 60 sts. With US 6 and Color A, pick up 57 sts along underside of chain, leaving extra chains to be removed later. Work the 138 rows of **Left Front Chart**, shaping neck as shown on chart.

## RIGHT FRONT

With G crochet hook and waste yarn, loosely chain approximately 60 sts. With US 6 and Color A, pick up 57 sts along underside of chain, leaving extra chains to be removed later. Work the 138 rows of **Right Front Chart**, shaping neck as shown on chart.

## SLEEVES

With US 5 and Color B, CO 51 sts. Work in st st for 6 rows, ending with RS facing for next row.

**Next Row (RS):** K2, *yo, k2tog**; rep from * to ** to last st; end, k1.
**Next Row (WS):** Purl.

Work in st st for 6 rows.

Work the 19 rows of **Sleeve Cuff Chart**.

Change to US 6 and work in st st, **AND AT SAME TIME**, inc 1 st at beg and end of next row, then every 3rd row 22 times (97 sts on needle), then every 4th row 6 times (109 sts on needle). Work without further shaping until sleeve measures 14" above sleeve cuff. BO.

### JOIN SHOULDERS AND SEW SIDE SEAMS

Sew shoulders tog. Sew side seams to 2" above provisional cast-on.

### BOTTOM BORDER

With US 5 and Color D, pick up bottom sts as you remove cast-on (be sure you have 225 sts on needle; dec if necessary). Work the 19 rows of **Bottom Border Chart**. Change to Color B and work in st st for 5 rows. Change to US 5.

**Next Row (RS):** K1, *yo, k2tog**; rep from * to ** to end of row.
**Next Row (WS):** Purl.

Work in st st for 5 rows. BO. Fold along picot and sew to inside.

### FINISHING

Place markers 11" down from shoulder seams on front and back and sew sleeves to armhole edge between markers. Sew sleeve seams, turning cuff at picot and sewing to inside. Sew rem side seams.

### COLLAR

With US 5 and Color A, RS facing, pick up 28 sts up right neck edge, 37 sts along back of neck and 28 sts down left neck edge (93 sts on needle). Purl 1 row. Work the 10 rows of **Collar Chart**. Change to Color B and work in st st for 4 rows.

**Next Row (RS):** K1, *yo, k2tog**; rep from * to ** to end of row.

Work in st st for 5 rows. Work in k1, p1 rib for 1½". BO. Fold collar at picot edge and sew to inside.

### FRONT BORDERS

With US 5 and Color A, RS facing, pick up 110 sts along left border. Work in st st for 7 rows. BO. Rep for right border.

Weave in ends. Block to finished measurements.

## Sleeve Cuff Chart

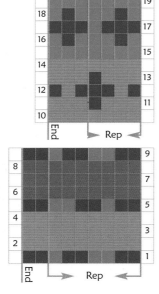

## Bottom Border Chart

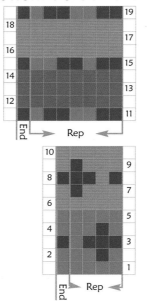

## Collar Chart

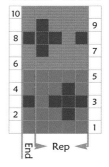

## Color Key

- Maroon (595)
- Plum (585)
- Port Wine (293)
- Rust (578)

# cosmos jacket

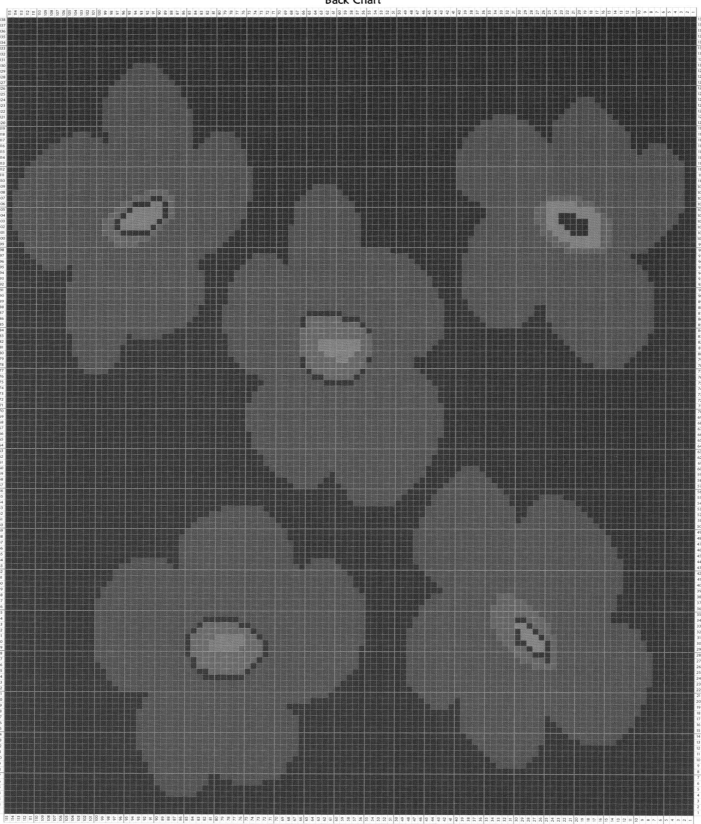

Right Front Chart

Beg Neck
Shaping
for Left
Front

Beg Neck
Shaping
for Right
Front

**Left Front Chart**

# cosmos vest

*nadine shapiro*

---

## MATERIALS

**YARN:** Jamieson's Shetland Double Knitting - 50 (50, 75, 75) grams of Maroon (595); 50 (50, 75, 75) grams of Plum (585); 100 (125, 125, 150) grams of Port Wine (293); and 50 (50, 50, 75) grams of Rust (578).
**NEEDLES:** 20" circular US 3 (3.25 mm) and 32" circular US 5 (3.75 mm), *or correct needles to obtain gauge.*
**ACCESSORIES:** Stitch holders.

## MEASUREMENTS

**CHEST:** 32 (36, 40, 44)".
**LENGTH TO ARMHOLE:** 12½ (13, 13, 13½)".
**ARMHOLE DEPTH:** 8½ (9, 10, 10½)".
**LENGTH:** 21 (22, 23, 24)".

## GAUGE

On US 5 in **Chart**: 24 sts and 32 rows = 4".

---

## ABOUT CHARTS

Read odd-numbered (RS) rows from right to left and even-numbered (WS) rows from left to right.

## BACK

With US 3 and Port Wine, CO 86 (98, 110, 122) sts.

**Row 1 (WS):** P2, ([k1, p2] 28 (32, 36, 40) times).
**Row 2 (RS):** K2, ([p1, k2] 28 (32, 36, 40) times).

Rep Rows 1-2 until piece measures 2½ (2½, 2½, 2½)" from CO edge, ending with WS facing for next row:

**Next Row (WS) (Inc): 1st Size:** P1, m1, p1; ([k1, p2, k1, p2, k1, p1, m1, p1] 9 times); end k1, p2 (96 sts on needle). **2nd Size:** P2, k1, p2; ([k1, p2, k1, p2, k1, p1, m1, p1] 10 times); end k1, p2 (108 sts on needle). **3rd Size:** ([P2, k1, p2, k1, p2, k1, p1, m1, p1] 10 times) (120 sts on needle). **4th Size:** P2, k1, p2, k1 ([p2, k1, p2, k1, p2, k1, p1, m1, p1] 10 times); end k1, p2, k1, p2 (132 sts on needle).

Change to US 5 and work **Chart** until piece measures 12½ (13, 13, 13½)" from CO edge, ending with RS facing for next row.

## SHAPE ARMHOLES

BO 4 (4, 6, 7) sts at beg of next 2 rows, 3 (3, 3, 3) sts at beg of next 2 rows, 2 (2, 2, 2) sts at beg of next 2 rows, then dec 1 (1, 1, 1) st at beg and end of next 6 (6, 6, 6) rows. Work without further shaping on rem 72 (84, 92, 102) sts until piece measures 21 (22, 23, 24)" from CO edge, ending with RS facing for next row.

**Next Row (RS):** Work 19 (24, 27, 31) sts and place on holder for right shoulder; work 34 (36, 38, 40) sts and place on holder for back neck; work 19 (24, 27, 31) sts and place on holder for left shoulder.

## FRONT

Work same as for back until piece measures 12½ (13, 13, 13½)" from CO edge, ending with RS facing for next row.

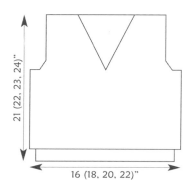

21 (22, 23, 24)"

16 (18, 20, 22)"

# cosmos vest

## SHAPE ARMHOLES & SHAPE NECK

**Next Row (RS):** BO 4 (4, 6, 7) sts; work rem 92 (104, 114, 125) sts.

**Next Row (WS):** BO 4 (4, 6, 7) sts; work 43 (49, 53, 58) sts; work 2 sts and place on holder; work rem 43 (49, 53, 58) sts.

Turn, and working each side separately, BO 3 (3, 3, 3) sts at armhole edge 1 (1, 1, 1) time, 2 (2, 2, 2) sts at armhole edge 1 (1, 1, 1) time, then dec 1 (1, 1, 1) st at armhole edge 3 (3, 3, 3) times. <u>ALSO</u> <u>AT</u> <u>SAME</u> <u>TIME</u>, dec at neck edge 1 st every 3rd row 16 (17, 18, 19) times. Work without further shaping on rem 19 (24, 27, 31) sts until piece measures 21 (22, 23, 24)" from CO edge. Place sts on holders for shoulders.

## JOIN SHOULDERS

With RS's facing, join shoulders using 3-needle bind-off method.

## ARMBANDS

With US 3 and Port Wine, RS facing, beg at underarm, pick up 110 (116, 128, 134) sts evenly around armhole edge.

**Row 1 (WS):** *P2, k1**; rep from * to **; end p2.
**Row 2 (RS):** *K2, p2**; rep from * to **; end k2.

Rep Rows 1-2 until armband measures 1 (1, 1, 1)". BO.

## NECKBAND

With US 3 and Port Wine, RS facing, beg at right shoulder, k34 (36, 38, 40) sts from back neck holder, pick up 52 (54, 57, 63) down left neck edge, place marker, knit 2 (2, 2, 2) sts from holder, place marker, pick up 51 (55, 57, 62) sts up right neck edge (139 (147, 154, 167) sts on needle). Join and work in the rnd as follows:

**Rnd 1: 1st Size:** ([K2, p1] to 2 sts before marker); ssk, slip marker, k2, slip marker, k2tog; ([p1, k2] to last st); p1. **2nd Size:** ([K2, p1] to 3 sts before marker); k1, ssk, slip marker, k2, slip marker, k2tog, k1; ([p1, k2] to last st); p1. **3rd Size:** ([K2, p1] to 2 sts before marker); ssk, slip marker, k2, slip marker, k2tog; ([p1, k2] to last st); p1. **4th Size:** ([K2, p1] to 4 sts before marker); k2, ssk, slip marker, k2, slip marker, k2tog, k2; ([p1, k2] to last st); p1.

Continuing rib as set and working left- and right-slanting dec's before 1st marker and after 2nd marker on every rnd, work until neckband measures 1 (1, 1, 1)". BO.

## FINISHING

Sew side seams and armbands at underarms. Weave in ends. Block to finished measurements.

## Chart

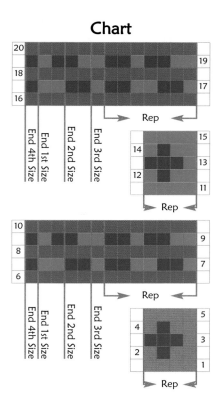

## Color Key

| | |
|---|---|
| ■ | Maroon (595) |
| ■ | Plum (585) |
| ■ | Port Wine (293) |
| ■ | Rust (578) |

# windowpanes pullover

*carol lapin*

## MATERIALS
YARN: Jamieson's Shetland Double Knitting - 550 (650) grams of Color A, Seaweed (253); 100 (125) grams of Color B, Black (999).
NEEDLES: 16" and 40" circular US 4 (3.5 mm) and 40" circular US 6 (4 mm), *or correct needles to obtain gauge.*
ACCESSORIES: Stitch holders. One 1" button.

## MEASUREMENTS
CHEST: 68 (68)".
BACK LENGTH: 23¾ (28¼)".
FRONT LENGTH: 21½ (26)".
SLEEVE LENGTH: 10 (10)".

## GAUGE
On US 6 in st st: 23 sts and 30 rows = 4".

## CHECKERBOARD PATTERN I (COLLAR)
Row 1 (RS): *K2B, k2A**; rep from * to **; end k2B.
Row 2 (WS): *P2B, p2A**; rep from * to **; end p2B.
Row 3 (RS): *K2A, k2B**; rep from * to **; end k2A.
Row 4 (WS): *P2A, p2B**; rep from * to **; end p2A.

Rep Rows 1-4.

## CHECKERBOARD PATTERN II (CUFFS)
Row 1 (RS): *K2A, k2B**; rep from * to **; end k1A.
Row 2 (WS): P1A, *p2B, p2A**; rep from * to **.
Row 3 (RS): *K2B, k2A**; rep from * to **; end k1B.
Row 4 (WS): P1B, *p2A, p2B**; rep from * to **.

Rep Rows 1-4.

## BACK
With US 4 and Color B, CO 197 (197) sts.

Rows 1, 3 & 5 (RS): With Color A, ([p1, k1] 3 times), p1; *with Color B, k1; with Color A ([p1, k1] 6 times), p1**; rep from * to ** 12 (12) times; with Color B, k1; with Color A, ([p1, k1] 3 times), p1.

Rows 2, 4 & 6 (WS): Knit the knit sts and purl the purl sts as they face you, keeping continuity of color sequence as established.

Change to US 6, and work in st st for 12 (12) rows, keeping continuity of color sequence.

*Next Row (RS): With Color B, knit. Break yarn and slide all sts to other end of needle. Next row will be a RS row.

Beg with a RS row, work 16 (16) rows in st st, working color sequence as before.**

Rep from * to ** until there are 10 (12) squares vertically, plus 6 (6) more rows, ending with RS facing for next row.

## SHAPE NECK
Next Row (RS): Work 78 (78) sts, BO 41 (41) sts, work 78 (78) sts.

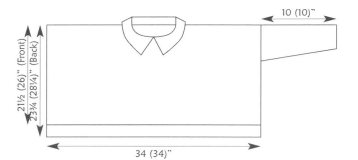

Working each side separately, work 1 (1) more row. Place shoulder sts on holders.

## FRONT
Work same as for back until there are 8 (10) squares vertically. Next row will be the row that is all Color B.

**Next Row (RS):** With Color B, k92 (92) sts and place on holder; k13 (13) sts and place on holder for front neck; k92 (92) sts. Break yarn and slide all sts to other end of needle.

Working each side separately, and keeping continuity of color sequence, BO 2 (2) sts at neck edge twice, then dec 1 st at neck edge every other row 10 (10) times. Place rem 78 (78) sts on holder for shoulder.

## JOIN SHOULDERS
With RS's facing, join shoulders using 3-needle bind-off method.

## NECK ROLL
With US 4, RS facing, beg at left shoulder seam, pick up 26 (26) sts down left neck edge; from front neck holder, k5, k2tog, k6 (12 (12) sts rem); pick up 26 (26) sts up right neck edge; pick up 45 (45) sts along back neck edge (109 (109) sts on needle). Mark beg of rnd, join, and purl 6 (6) rnds. BO.

**NOTE:** When picking up sts for **Collar** (below), *pick up along WS of original neck edge, omitting the 6 purl rows knitted for the* **Neck Roll**—*these 6 purl rows should be left free to roll forward and hide the picked-up* **Collar** *edge.*

## COLLAR
With US 6, WS facing, beg at center front, pick up 34 (34) sts up right neck edge, 46 (46) sts along back neck edge, and 34 (34) sts down left neck edge (114 (114) sts on needle). Purl 1 (1) row. Work the 4 rows of **Checkerboard Pattern I** 6 (6) times, **AND AT SAME TIME**, inc 1 st at beg and end of every other row, working pattern into inc'd sts. With Color B, BO.

## SLEEVES
Beg at 3½ (3½) squares down from shoulder seams, with US 6, RS facing *(matching colors to body)*, ([with Color A, pick up 13 (13) sts; with Color B, pick up 1 (1) st] 6 (6) times); with Color A, pick up 13 (13) sts (97 (97) sts on needle).

Keeping continuity of color sequence, work 9 (9) rows, **AND AT SAME TIME**, dec 1 st at beg and end of every 4th row.

***Next Row (RS):** With Color B, knit. Break yarn and slide all sts to other end of needle. Next row will be a RS row.

Beg with a RS row, and continuing dec's as set, work 16 (16) rows in st st, working color sequence as before.****

Rep from * to ** until 65 (65) sts rem and sleeve measures approx. 10 (10)".

## CUFFS
Work the 4 rows of **Checkerboard Pattern II** twice. Change to US 4 and Color B and work 2 (2) rows in st st. BO.

## FINISHING
Match pattern at side seams, leaving bottom square of back unsewn (back is one pattern square longer than front). With Color B, work single crochet along edge of unsewn squares. Sew sleeve seams. With Color B, work single crochet along edge of collar from one point to center front to other point. Sew button to center of neck roll.

# Abbreviations

**alt** = alternate

**beg** = beginning

**BO** = bind off

**CC** = contrast color

**cn** = cable needle

**CO** = cast on

**dec** = decrease(ing)

**foll** = follow(ing)

**GS** = garter stitch

**inc** = increase(ing)

**k** = knit

**kfb** = knit into front and back of st (inc)

**k1b** = knit through back loop

**k2tog** = knit 2 sts together

**k2togtbl** = knit 2 sts together through back loop

**m1** = make 1 st (inc) - lift running thread between st just worked and next st and knit into back of loop

**m1p** = make 1 st (inc) purl - lift running thread between st just worked and next st and purl into front of loop

**kwise** = knitwise (as if to knit)

**MC** = main color

**p** = purl

**p2tog** = purl 2 sts together

**patt** = pattern

**psp** = p1 and slip to left-hand needle; pass next st over it; return to right-hand needle

**psso** = pass slipped st over st just knitted

**p3sso** = pass 3 slipped sts over st just knitted

**pwise** - purlwise (as if to purl)

**rem** = remaining

**rep** = repeat

**rnd** = round

**RS** = right side

**sl** = slip

**sl1wyib** = with yarn in back, slip 1 st pwise

**sl1wyif** = with yarn in front, slip 1 st pwise

**ssk** = sl 2 sts (one at a time) kwise; with left-hand needle, knit these two sts tog through front of sts

**ssp** = sl 2 sts kwise (one at a time); return both sts to left-hand needle; k2togtbl

**st(s)** = stitch(es)

**st st** = stockinette stitch

**tbl** = through back loop

**tog** = together

**WS** = wrong side

**yo** = (inc) yarn over needle

# Skill Levels

*Beginner*      *Intermediate*       *Expert*

Jamieson's Shetland wool is distributed in North America by **Simply** *Shetland* and can be found at these fine stores:

ALASKA
Anchorage
Knitting Frenzy
800-478-8322

ARKANSAS
Little Rock
Simply Shetland at Handworks Gallery
501-664-6300
www.handworksgallery.com

CALIFORNIA
Los Altos
Simply Shetland at Uncommon Threads
650-941-1815

Mendocino
Simply Shetland at Mendocino Yarn Shop
888-530-1400
www.mendocinoyarnshop.com

Oakland
Article Pract
510-652-7435
www.articlepract.com

Simply Shetland at The Knitting Basket
510-339-6295
www.theknittingbasket.com

Sebastopol
Simply Shetland at Knitting Workshop
707-824-0699

COLORADO
Colorado Springs
Needleworks by Holly Berry
719-636-1002
www.hollyberryhouse.com

CONNECTICUT
Avon
Simply Shetland at Wool Connection
800-933-9655
www.woolconnection.com

Deep River
Yarns Down Under
860-526-9986
www.yarnsdownunder.com

Glastonbury
Village Wool
860-633-0898

Newington
Simply Shetland at Needleworks
800-665-0277
www.needleworksonline.com

Mystic
Mystic River Yarns
860-536-4305

New Preston
The Village Sheep, LLC
860-354-5442

Old Saybrook
Saybrook Yarn
860-388-3415
www.saybrookyarn.net

Stratford
Janet Kemp, LLC
203-386-9276

Woodbridge
The Yarn Barn
203-389-5117
www.theyarnbarn.com

GEORGIA
Roswell
Simply Shetland at Cast-On Cottage
770-998-3483

ILLINOIS
Chicago
Knitting Workshop
773-929-5776
www.knittingworkshop.com

Des Plaines
Mosaic Yarn Studio, Ltd.
847-390-1013
mosaicyarn@aol.com

Lake Forest
Simply Shetland at The Keweenaw Shepherd
847-295-9524

INDIANA
Fort Wayne
Cass Street Depot
888-420-2292
www.cassstreetdepot.com

Valparaiso
Simply Shetland at Sheep's Clothing
219-462-1700

KANSAS
Lawrence
Yarn Barn
785-842-4333
www.yarnbarn-ks.com

MAINE
Camden
Simply Shetland at Stitchery Square
207-236-9773
www.stitcherysquare.com

Hallowell
Water Street Yarns
207-622-5500

MARYLAND
Bethesda
Simply Shetland at Yarns International
800-927-6728
www.yarnsinternational.com

MASSACHUSETTS
Brookfield
Simply Shetland at KnitWitts
877-877-KNIT
www.knitwitts.com

Brookline
A Good Yarn
617-731-4900
www.agoodyarn.biz

Cambridge
Simply Shetland at Woolcott & Company
617-547-2837
www.woolcottandco.com

Cohasset
Creative Stitch
781-383-0667

Concord
Needle Arts of Concord
978-371-0424
www.needle-arts.com

Harwich Port
Simply Shetland at Adventures in Knitting
508-432-3700
www.adventuresinknitting.com

Lenox
Colorful Stitches
800-413-6111
www.colorful-stitches.com

Lexington
Simply Shetland at Wild & Woolly Studio
781-861-7717
wwoolly@aol.com

Needham
Creative Warehouse
781-444-9341
creativewarehouse@cs.com

Northampton
Northampton Wools
413-586-4331

Webs
800-367-9327
www.yarn.com

Plymouth
Knitting Treasures
508-747-2500

South Hamilton
Cranberry Fiber Arts
978-468-3871

Vineyard Haven
Heath Hen Quilt Shop
508-693-6730
www.heathhen.com

Walpole
Dee's Nimble Needles
508-668-8499

MICHIGAN
Birmingham
The Knitting Room
248-540-3623
www.knittingroom.com

Grosse Point
The Wool & the Floss
313-882-9110
www.thewoolandthefloss.com

Lansing
Simply Shetland at Threadbear Fiber Arts Studio
517-703-9276
www.threadbearfiberarts.com

Marquette
Town Folk Gallery
906-225-9010
www.townfolkgallery.com

Tawas Bay
Tawas Bay Yarn Company
989-362-4463
misso@chartermi.net

**MINNESOTA**

**Duluth**
Simply Shetland at Yarn Harbor
218-724-6432
www.yarnharbor.com

**Minneapolis**
Simply Shetland at Linden Hills Yarns
612-929-1255

Simply Shetland at Needlework Unlimited
888-925-2454
www.needleworkunlimited.com

**St. Paul**
Simply Shetland at Three Kittens Yarn
Shoppe
651-457-4969

Simply Shetland at The Yarnery
651-222-5793

**White Bear Lake**
Simply Shetland at A Sheepy Yarn Shoppe
800-480-5462
www.sheepyyarn.com

**NEW HAMPSHIRE**

**Concord**
Simply Shetland at The Elegant Ewe
603-226-0066
www.elegantewe.com

**Exeter**
Simply Shetland at Charlotte's Web
603-778-1417
www.charlotteswebyarns.com

**Laconia**
The Yarn Shop & Fibres
603-528-1221
www.yarnshoponline.com

**NEW JERSEY**

**Lambertville**
Simply Shetland at Simply Knit
609-397-7101
www.simplyknit.com

**Sparta**
Yarn Loft
973-383-6667

**NEW YORK**

**Rochester**
The Village Yarn Shop
585-454-6064

**NORTH CAROLINA**

**Raleigh**
Great Yarns
919-832-3599
www.great-yarns.com

**OHIO**

**Columbus**
Simply Shetland at Wolfe Fiber Arts
614-487-9980
www.wolfefiberarts.com

**Toledo**
FiberWorks Knitting & Weaving
419-389-1821

**OREGON**

**Ashland**
Simply Shetland at The Web-sters
800-482-9801
www.yarnatwebsters.com

**Carlton**
Simply Shetland at Woodland Woolworks
800-547-3725
www.woolworks.com

**Eugene**
The Knit Shop
541-434-0430
www.knit-shop.com

**Lake Oswego**
Molehill Farm
503-697-9554
www.molehillfarm.com

**Portland**
Simply Shetland at The Yarn Garden
503-239-7950
www.yarngarden.net

**PENNSYLVANIA**

**Chambersburg**
Simply Shetland at The Yarn Basket
888-976-2758
www.yarnbasketpa.com

**Kennett Square**
Wool Gathering
610-444-8236
knit@woolgathering.com

**Philadelphia**
Rosie's Yarn Cellar
215-977-9276
www.rosiesyarncellar.com

Tangled Web
215-242-1271
www.tangledweb.com

**RHODE ISLAND**

**Providence**
Simply Shetland at A Stitch Above
800-949-5648
www.knitri.com

**Wickford**
And the Beadz Go On...
401-268-3899

**VIRGINIA**

**Burke**
The Yarn Barn
800-762-5274
www.geocities.com/theyarnbarnonline

**Dillwyn**
Yarn Barn of Andersonville
800-850-6008
www.yarnbarn.com

**WASHINGTON**

**Bainbridge Island**
Churchmouse Yarns & Teas
206-780-2686
www.churchmouseyarns.com

**Kennewick**
Sheep's Clothing
509-734-2484

**Kent**
Simply Shetland at The Two Swans Yarns
888-830-8269
www.twoswansyarn.com

**Olympia**
Canvas Works
360-352-4481

**Renton**
Knittery
800-742-3565

**Seattle**
Hilltop Yarn & Needlepoint
206-282-5330

So Much Yarn...
800-443-0727
www.somuchyarn.com

Simply Shetland at The Weaving Works
888-524-1221
www.weavingworks.com

**WISCONSIN**

**Appleton**
Simply Shetland at Jane's Knitting Hutch
920-954-9001
www.janesknittinghutch.com

**Delafield**
Simply Shetland at The Knitting Ark
262-646-2464

**Elm Grove**
The Yarn House
262-786-5660

**Madison**
Lakeside Fibers
608-257-2999
www.lakesidefibers.com

**Milwaukee**
Simply Shetland at Ruhama's Yarn
& Needlepoint
414-332-2660
www.ruhamas.com

**Neenah**
Yarns by Design
888-559-2767
www.yarnsbydesign.com

**Verona**
The Sow's Ear
608-848-2755
www.knitandsip.com

**CANADA/Ontario**

**Ancaster**
The Needle Emporium
905-648-1994
www.needleemporium.com

**Kingston**
The Wool Room
800-449-5868 (in Canada)
613-544-9544
info@woolroom.on.ca

**"Simply Shetland at"** stores carry a wide selection of Jamieson's wools.

Editorial Director     **David Codling**

Editor & Graphic Design     **Gregory Courtney**

Assistant to the Editor     **Diane Brown**

Photography     **Kathryn Martin**

Illustrations     **Molly Eckler**

Garments Modeled by     **Gabrielle Thorpe, Nate Barker, Cameron Thorpe, Shelley Alger & "Bella"**

Makeup & Hair Styling     **Kira Lee**

Clothing Stylist     **Betsy Westman**

Knitting     **Bernadette St. Amant**

Buttons     **Muench Buttons** (www.muenchyarns.com)

Location Thanks     **The City of Mendocino, California, The Mendocino Hotel, Sticks**

Special Thanks     **Annelle Karlstad, Mendocino Yarn Shop**

Color Reproduction & Printing     **Global Interprint, Inc.**

Published By     **Simply Shetland** (www.simplyshetland.net)

Distributed By     **Unicorn Books and Crafts, Inc.** (www.unicornbooks.com)

Printed in Hong Kong

ISBN
**0-9752931-0-9**

1 2 3 4 5 6 7 8 9 10